T0116962

Sunday Morning
Volume 1

Inspirational Sermon
Guide for Busy Pastors

Dr. Richie Bell, Jr.

FOREWORD: Dr. Leonard Rhone, Sr.

iUniverse, Inc.
Bloomington

Sunday Morning Volume 1
Inspirational Sermon Guide for Busy Pastors

iUniverse books may be ordered through booksellers or by contacting:

iUniverse
1663 Liberty Drive
Bloomington, IN 47403
www.iuniverse.com
1-800-Authors (1-800-288-4677)

ISBN: 978-1-4620-1196-4 (sc)
ISBN: 978-1-4620-1197-1 (ebk)

Printed in the United States of America

iUniverse rev. date: 04/18/2011

Foreword

S eldom are we given the opportunity to peer into the heart and soul of a person who has been given an awesome assignment from God. Yet in **"Sunday Morning" Volume One** we are given a glimpse into the inner thoughts and struggles of a true prophet of the kingdom of God. Dr. Richie Bell, Jr. goes with his work where few are willing to go. He takes us into the soul of the preacher and causes us to see that there are many moves on the chessboard before one can say, "Checkmate."

When we accept the call of God first to preach God's Word and then to pastor God's people, we have no idea where that will take us. Preaching is the vehicle we use to communicate the message, by pastoring is the art of leadership, enabling people to get to the places God has purposed for them. Dr. Bell makes it clear that the pastor's burden is heard in his preaching and the preacher's struggle is felt in pastoring. However, he affirms that the Word of God is the answer and hope for the church and its individual members. He is not one who would replace preaching with fancy serendipities; he confidently affirms that it is through preaching that vision is seen, understood, and embraced.

I hope that all who read this work will begin to sense what it takes to craft a sermon. I hope that you will see that only as the preacher bares his soul, with its fears and hopes, can a sermon emerge. A sermon is not; three points and a poem; nor is it just a verse-by-verse discussion; it is a window into the soul of the preacher who sits with God.

As you begin to read the pages, I believe you will find it will be difficult to stop reading. When you have completed this book, you will find you have 25 recipes for spiritual guidance. You will be able to identify the ingredients needed to battle and survive the turmoil of conflict and evil present in our communities and world. No doubt, it will be a book that you will want to keep in easy reach to reference over and over.

Again, I express my appreciation to Dr. Bell for the privilege and opportunity to offer my comments. This book may not make the national headlines as a bestseller and it may not be reviewed on the morning news' shows or by the Oprah Winfrey Book Club. However, when you have completed the book, I know you will join me in feeling the fire of inspiration and concern for the acts of ungodly behavior that are constant in our communities.

Read this book. Let others know about the 25 **"never-fail"** recipes for survival and challenging the **Angel of Evil -Satan.**

Dr. Leonard Rhone, Sr.

Oakland Baptist Church

Shreveport, Louisiana

Introduction

S unday Morning Volume 1, Inspirational Sermon Guide is the
best investment you won't regret. It's loaded with phenomenal
sermons, and tremendous outlines. This sermon guide is guaranteed
to instantly grab the attention of the congregation, enhance your personal
biblical knowledge, and increase attendance of the membership.

This guide is not intended to suffice for Pastoral sermon preparation.
It's only intended use is to assist when needed to facilitate greater
efficiency in sermon preparation. Sermon preparation follows the study
and precedes the delivery of the message. Needless to say, the design and
writing of the sermon is at the heart of producing and preaching a good
sermon. I truly believe that **Sunday Morning Volume 1, Inspirational
Sermon Guide** will help you reach that pinnacle. There is no doubt that
you will be energized, enlighten, and encouraged with the use of this
guide.

Contrary to what some churchgoers may think, Pastors are busy. Pastors
do more than teach and preach. Today's busy Pastors are expected to lead
their congregations, guide planning efforts, administer church business,
visit the sick, provide counseling, and much more. It's understandable
that many Pastors search for sermon outlines to help them in their sermon
preparation. For those who may object to prepared sermon outlines from
an outside resource! Sermon outlines are not full sermons. They are merely
tools to help the Pastor in his preparation.

Pastors wanting to use these outlines must flesh them out further through additional Bible study, prayer, and research. Pastors should also feel free to add their own personal stories and observations. They must also add their own conclusion, something appropriate to their personality and congregation.

It is my continued hope that **Sunday Morning Volume 1, Inspirational Sermon Guide** provide inspiration, provoke new thoughts for sermons, and remind us all of what is eternally important. It is my desire that even the experienced expositor, as he works his way through this guide, will be refreshed and reminded of helpful principles and truths.

Dr. Richie Bell, Jr.
Author

Acknowledgment

Thanks to each of you who supported me to write this pastor's guide. I would like to thank my pastor Dr. Leonard Rhone Sr., pastor of Oakland Baptist Church, Dr. Leon Richmond, pastor of New Light Baptist Church, Dr. T.C.L. Ward (President), and staff of Inter-Baptist Theological Seminary Inc., Dr. Milton McGrew (Dean), and staff of United Theological Seminary and Bible College, Dr. Rickey LJ Moore Sr., pastor of Sunrise Baptist Church.

I would like to express a special thanks to my entire biological family for their continued support. To the incredible members of the Pilgrim Travelers Missionary Baptist Church of Shreveport, Louisiana; whom I have served for several years, thanks for your support.

This Busy Pastor's Sermon Guide, is an inspiration which expresses my deepest sympathy, compassion and devotion for preaching the uncompromising Gospel of Jesus Christ.

Effective Preaching Tips

I. *Plan Ahead-* Most pastors can block out at least two full days each month for sermon planning and preparation. Take that time to prayerfully identify topics and/or passages, and then develop outlines accordingly.

II. *Read and Listen to Other Sermons Regularly -* Use drive time or down time to review sermons by other pastors. Include classic sermons. Any pastor can learn from great preachers of the past, such as B.W. Smith, W. Leo Daniels, or Ceasar A.W. Clark, Sr.

III. *Keep Eyes and Ears Open for Illustrations and Quotes -* Busy pastors should always be on the lookout for great stories, quotations and anecdotes. These can be personal or drawn from other sources (such as the news, history books, or television). Keeping a file of ready-to-go, personally collected illustrations and quotes will help immensely when it comes to sermon preparation.

IV. *Select a Passage and Ask the "W" Questions -* Pastors can take any passage (Genesis 1, Psalm 23, I Corinthians 13, etc.), break it down into topical sections, and then ask the "W" questions (who, what, where, when, why) about each section. Going through this exercise will generate plenty of sermon material!

V. *Capture the Congregation Attention-*Incorporate an attention getting introduction that leads into the message. The introduction can be a story, joke, series of statistics, etc. Just make sure the introduction compliments and leads into the message.

VI.   *Explain the need for the Sermon*- Don't let the congregation wonder why such a message is being preached. They need to see right away why this sermon is important.

VII.   *Pace Yourself*- Don't rush and take time to explain those biblical passages you choose to read.

VIII.   *Dramatization*-Expound and dramatize each sub-point, adding another illustration, quote, story, etc.

IX.   *Express Personal Testimonials*-Weave in personal experiences and observations.

X.   *Wrap Up*-Close with an appeal that's applicable to your congregation.

Table of Contents

Chapter 1

⁓✳⁓

I Got the Pastor's Back

(1 Kings 19:21 KJV)

And he returned back from him, and took a yoke of oxen, and slew them, and boiled their flesh with the instruments of the oxen, and gave unto the people, and they did eat. Then he arose, and went after Elijah, and ministered unto him.

Nearly nine centuries before Christ, Ahab, king of Israel, married the daughter of the pagan king of a neighboring country. During the 22 years of his reign, the name of his wife became a household word more accurately, a household curse! Yes Jezebel was her named. This manipulative woman Jezebel manipulated everyone she met and repeatedly defied the Word of God spoken through the prophet Elijah. Jezebel always got her way and woe unto those unfortunate enough to get in her way! Her happiness depended on being on the top of others; even to this day, she abides with the record of Scripture as an embodiment of a power-hungry and unreachable heart of animosity and outraged.

In the text we read about Elijah, he is larger-than-life. He is faithful, confident, and authoritative. He is able to bring about miracles through prayer, even raising the dead and calling fire down from heaven. He is able to confront a powerful king and accuse him of sin, and he dares to challenge a large crowd of people who follow the god Baal. In this chapter we find the prophet Elijah an intimidated, suicidal, self doubting yet self-righteous whiner who is on the run.

God spoke encouraging words to Elijah the Tishbite the prophet "*Yet I have left me seven thousand in Israel, all the knees which have not bowed unto Baal, and every mouth which hath not kissed him*" (1 Kings 19:18), at a time when he felt very lonely and thought he was about to die because of ministerial depression.

While these accounts shock us, they also serve to help us. How? They remind us that depression is a common experience. It is something that often happens in life. In other words, if you go through a time of depression, you are not alone. Notice these facts concerning depression.

- Depression affects all classes, races, ages, groups and genders of people.
- 17.6 million Americans will deal with some form of depression this year.
- One out of every five Americans can expect to deal with depression in their lifetime.
- The rate of clinical depression is twice that of men. Statistics teach that one person out of every seven will need some form of professional help in dealing with depression in their lifetime.
- The National Institute of Mental Health estimated that depression cost the nation between $30-$44 billion in 1990. In addition, over 2 million work days are lost each year due to depression.
- Depression is not something to mess with! If you are dealing with depression, get help!

Listen to why Elijah was so depressed and tired of this intrusive oxymoron!

Jezebel was a callous iniquitous woman. During the reign of Ahab, Elijah exfoliated 450 of their false prophets. So, Jezebel in rage sent a personal message to Elijah," *So let the gods do to me, and more also, if I make not thy life as the life of one of them by to morrow about this time*" (1 Kings 19:2). Jezebel intended to kill him that very day or the next day at the latest.

Instead of Elijah standing, like he did before Ahab and the prophets of Baal, Elijah tucks his tail and get out of town. Elijah overcame all the obstacles that he faced in the pass. He now decides to run from the presence of Jezebel.

In the past Elijah had faced and survived, dry Brook University, He faced the empty barrel of not enough, He faced the dead boy who escaped the hands of death, and He faced the prophets of Baal and the lack of rain.

Elijah saw the Lord close the heavens and there was no rain upon his request for 3 ½ years, He saw the Lord replenish the meal barrel, He saw the Lord raise the boy, He saw the Lord consume the sacrifice upon Mount Carmel, He seen the Lord enable the prophet to destroy the false prophets and he runs from Jezreel to the southern border of Judah approximately 125 miles away from Jezebel. In the eyes of Elijah, Jezebel was fugitively obsolete at first, and perhaps an inconsiderable problem but that's not the ultimate issue here.

Listen! Ahab is all quite in this matter. He's not instructing his wife in this matter to leave this preacher alone, but tucks his tail between his legs.

I just want to interject a few thoughts right here. Jezebel is a typical domineering woman. Her actions prove this to be true. First, she made all the decisions in this matter. Secondly, she performed Ahab's job her way. Thirdly, she used scheming and intimidation tactics when she saw her defenseless husband (king of Israel) beginning to cave into any kind of pressure. Ahab, on the other hand is a true henpecked husband. He may have been the king, but Jezebel wore the crown in that castle! She was the boss, and he was her servant!

Elijah does that which is irrational and runs away from it all. I mean when you are kicked by a mule, stand up, stand still, watch the salvation of the Lord and just consider the source! When a carnal person kicks at your efforts and works that you've accomplished, just ignore them and carry on.

It is a danger to threaten the man of God especially the pastor. Rather if it's openly or discreetly. When the pastor is disturbed, and his feelings are damaged when people have pre-motives to make him seem powerless and challenges his administration, authority, affirmation and doctrinal views, somebody should to have common sense of concern to not only say, but show and tell others in-spite of our indifferences, "**I Got the Pastor's Back**!"

I like Elijah's response to Jezebel, even though he ran away on foot, and kept on running for more than a month he didn't run for the reasons we would expect. He honestly thought he was the last person in the country who truly loved and honored God, and if he was killed, there would be no one else left who would serve Him. In Elijah's day many people lost their faith, firmness and focus. But God still had His seven thousand who were committed to Him!

So, Elijah said *"I have been very jealous for the LORD God of hosts: because the children of Israel have forsaken thy covenant, thrown down thine altars, and slain thy prophets with the sword; and I, even I only, am left; and they seek my life, to take it away"* (1 Kings 19:14).

Elijah was in a bad situation and was extremely upset. He was in what we might call "a walk through a dark valley" of life, because of his people and out of love for God.

When Israel did fall as a nation, those "seven thousand" were conquered. When captivity happened, they went into captivity, too. We as believers must understand, bad things do happen to good people, and when they do, God uses those circumstances to bring us even closer to Christ who sacrificed his life for us. The "bad" times changes us and draws us closer to Him.

The Prophet Elijah journeyed into the wilderness. He sits down under a Juniper tree; throws in the towel and asks God to take his life. If he really wanted to die, why didn't he just stay in Jezreel and let Jezebel take care of it for him? Elijah had reached rock bottom. He sat down and he gave up. Elijah felt that life was no longer worth living.

Elijah goes upon Mount Horeb. This mountain was a place of great significance for the children of Israel. Here, Moses had met God by a burning bush. It was here that God had handed down His law to the people of Israel. Perhaps, Elijah went here so that he too might hear the voice of God. When he arrives he goes into a cave, and sits down to wait for God to speak.

The Lord's voice does come to the prophet in that cave. He asks Elijah this question:

"Elijah, what are you doing in a cave on Mount Horeb? Did I not send you to preach to my people Israel? Shouldn't you be in Israel leading my people in a great revival? I didn't call you to run to this cave and hide yourself away. I called you to stand before kings, to defy false gods and prophets and to be an example of righteousness for the people of Israel."

While Elijah stood in that cave on Mount Horeb, the Lord passed by. First, there was a great strong wind that rent the mountain, then an earthquake that shook the mountain to its foundation. After that there was a great fire. However, we are told that the Lord was in neither of these. After that, there was a still, small voice. What the earthquake and the fire could not do, the small still voice did. The infinite voice touched Elijah's heart!

Elijah is told to return to Israel; there, he is to anoint two kings and a prophet (**Elisha**). He is given an important assignment from the Lord. He is given evidence that the Lord is not finished with his life. Elisha was to be a companion to Elijah and would take Elijah's place when his ministry ended. I like the concluding words of this chapter, *"And he returned back from him, and took a yoke of oxen, and slew them, and boiled their flesh with the instruments of the oxen, and gave unto the people, and they did eat. Then he arose, and went after Elijah, and ministered unto him "*(1 Kings 19:21).

God knew that the burdens Elijah carried were too heavy for him to bear alone. So God gave him a confidant, a friend, a peer. He gave him Elisha one to walk beside him through the valleys and through the difficulties of life. Elisha can truly say, "**I Got the Pastor's Back!**"

Elijah ached for his people and loved His God. He grieved they had turned from God. In result God blessed him. As Elijah departed he found Elisha (1 Kings 19:19-21), who was to be his student, his friend, and eventually his successor. God's people are all around, but so often we do not recognize them for what they are worth.

Elijah's eyes were opened and he instantaneously saw someone just like himself. They may be different than we expect, just like the Bible is different from other books, but it is full of the Holy Spirit and so are God's people.

You know who they are. They eventually learn to laugh when things go wrong. "Bad" state of affairs brings them closer to God. They find love and forgiveness for those who harm them. They trust in God when everything goes wrong. They can praise God in everything you bring their way.

Look at him now! We find Elijah well on the road to recuperation. He is back, and he is serving God once again. The Lord's ministry in his life has delivered him from the threshold of death and of shipwreck. Moreover, many of you need that ministry today. You are on the verge of quitting on the Lord. You are discouraged and defeated. But God is the answer to all of your personal problems.

Chapter 2

⌐⌐⌐

God's Facebook Page

(Revelation 21:27 KJV)

And there shall in no wise enter into it any thing that defileth,
neither whatsoever worketh abomination, or maketh a lie:
but they which are written in the Lamb's book of life.

These days many people are excited and don't mind sharing their experiences with Facebook. Facebook is a website that serves as a free online community and connects people from all over the world. Originally, Facebook was only open to students of Harvard University, but eventually branched out to include all Ivy League schools, all college students, high schools, and eventually became a completely open service requiring only a valid email address.

It is estimated that the social network has more than 175 million active users and it's mostly used to help people meet, stay in contact, and learn more about each other. The widespread search features allow people to locate one another but requires approval from the user to maintain security by requesting the friend request acceptance.

Facebook includes the ability to upload and share an unlimited number of photographs, videos, and many more optional preferences.

While I was uploading some photos on to Facebook, I thought about the fact, just as we have a Facebook page more importantly, God also has a Facebook page. God's eyes are in every place watching the good and the evil as if the entire world in which we reside is only one page in His sight. So, I thought more in-depth concerning how we as common people become members on **"God's Facebook Page"** (The Lamb's Book of Life).

There are many faces in this book. They are listed by their names according to Apostle John.

"And I saw the dead, small and great, stand before God; and the books were opened: and another book was opened, which is the book of life: and the dead were judged out of those things which were written in the books, according to their works. And the sea gave up the dead which were in it; and death and hell delivered up the dead which were in them: and they were judged every man according to their works. And death and hell were cast into the lake of fire. This is the second death. And whosoever was not found written in the book of life was cast into the lake of fire" (Revelation 20:12-15).

In order to be listed in this book there are three requirements:
I. God's Facebook Page Requires Registration:
II. God's Facebook Page Requires Relationship:
III. God's Facebook Page Requires Reverence:

I. God's Facebook Page Requires Registration:

Many Facebook subscribers utilize Facebook to search for those whom they haven't seen in a while. Many of them desire to find distanced friends and relatives etc. The first thing you must do to subscribe to **God's Facebook Page**:

- **Register with Him before Recognition:**

On Facebook you must create a passcode. You must give your identity etc. And finally add a few photos of your face before utilizing the site.

If you want to know more about God and His Facebook page, you must register with Him, before you get to know Him. His passcode is not secretive. It's simple to login with Him!

Before He recognizes you, there's one important factor you must consider, *"Jesus answered and said unto him, Verily, verily, I say unto thee, Except a man be born again, he cannot see the kingdom of God"* (John 3:3). You must be born again, considering you've already been blood brought!

You must drop off sin on **Enough Blvd**, pick up salvation on **Righteous Lane**, and fill up with the Holy Ghost on **Sanctified Avenue**.

It is (He) God (the Theos), who **selected us**, through Jesus (the Logos), who **saved us**, byway of the Holy Ghost (the Paraclete), the third person of the God head Trinity who **seals us**.

As His **master** piece we must recognize Him as our **maker**, as His **creatures** he removes our **chrisom** stains, and as our **everlasting** God of **eternity**, it is He who **erases** our **errors**.

We are required as believers to be counted as being in the right standing with God, and to register spiritually with Him, before we receive His recognition, that's if we desire a spot on **"God's Facebook Page."**

II. God's Facebook Page Requires Relationship:

On Facebook, if you find someone you desire to become friends with or try to reunite with from the pass, you must request them and wait patiently to be accepted.

In order for God to accept you as a friend, you must show yourself to be friendly.

"A man that hath friends must shew himself friendly: and there is a friend that sticketh closer than a brother" (Proverbs 18:24).

Jesus is a true friend who sticks closer than a brother. Jesus is the first person to step in, when the whole world steps out, especially when trouble arises.

I'm reminded about a story of two men, these two men were hunting and suddenly one yelled and the other looked up to see a lion charging towards them. The first man started to hurriedly put on his tennis shoes and his friend anxiously asked, "What are you doing? Don't you know you can't outrun a lion?" the man replied "I don't have to outrun the lion. I just have to outrun you!"

That's the kind of friends most of us have. When the chips are down, they think of themselves only. A true friend always puts you first! Jesus loved us enough to put us first as His friend. If you seek Him you shall find Him.

It is God through Solomon, who expressed:

"I love them that love me; and those that seek me early shall find me" (Proverbs 8:17).

Whenever you desire to dialog with God, just send Him a friend request for His approval. If you send Him a spiritual friend request, covered by the atoning blood of His only begotten Son, He won't fail you nor ever turn your request down. Thank Jesus for His Blood!

- His Blood Released Us.
- His Blood Redeemed Us.
- His Blood Regenerated Us.
- His Blood Reminds Us.
- His Blood Washed Us.
- His Blood Cleansed Us.

- His Blood Justified Us.
- His Blood Sanctified Us.

Thank Jesus for His Blood!

III. God's Facebook Page Requires Reverence:

Many people on Facebook love to reverence themselves than others. Webster's defines reverence as: *honor or respect felt or shown for someone or something.*

God is looking upon this world acknowledging who's reverencing Him. We must keep in mind that God is not interested in us accomplishing great things for Him. He's interested in our personal relationship with him. We cannot serve God until our hearts are fixed on him, and our hearts cannot be fixed on him until we begin to surrender to him.

There is one thing that you must realize above all things before you praise Him. *"God is a Spirit: and they that worship him must worship him in spirit and in truth"* (John 4:24). This tells us by what mode God communicates with us. Since God is spirit, he communicates with us spiritually.

The next time you hear of someone speaking of Facebook, remind them that God has a Facebook page too! Remember He's watching the good and the evil. According to Apostle John; God as He sits on the throne in the third heaven. He has the Lamb's book of life, and explains to us the purity required of and in the New Jerusalem.

"And there shall in no wise enter into it any thing that defileth, neither whatsoever worketh abomination, or maketh a lie: but they which are written in the Lamb's book of life" (Revelation 21:27).

God has kept record book on every individual who has ever lived. In fact, out of those records, based on the light of revelation; we will all be justly judged out of it. It was in the context of the record books that we read, another book was opened, which was the book of life. In Revelation, that book is called the, "Lamb's Book of Life."

"And I saw the dead, small and great, stand before God; and the books were opened: and another book was opened, which is the book of life: and the dead were judged out of those things which were written in the books, according to their works" (Revelation 20:12).

Under the names of the saved are listed their perfections. What a glorious thought to contemplate! Jesus became sin for me, and I have become the righteousness of God in Him. We traded record books! He took mine to the cross and grave; I will take His to heaven!

Chapter 3

◦ᴖᴖᴖ◦

Let Jesus Have It

(John 6:9 KJV)

*There is a lad here, which have five barley loaves, and two
small fishes: but what are they among so many?*

The feeding of the five thousand is Jesus only miracle that is recorded in all four gospels. A comparison of all the accounts provides a more complete understanding than reading just one of the synoptic gospel accounts for the authenticity of the miracle.

The Holy Spirit moved upon each of these gospel writers. It moved upon Matthew who writes to the Jews, Mark who writes to the Romans, Luke who writes to the Greeks and John who writes to the world.

They all report that the same basic events happened. It's a story that is impossible to "spiritualize." It cannot be dismissed as a mere parable. It is reported to us as a historical event. Jesus truly did feed a large multitude of people with a few loaves of bread and a few small fish. This is what I like to call a "three piece fish dinner."

The Holy Spirit, the third person of the God head trinity has preserved this story for us so that we will learn to respond to the seemingly impossible situations of life by trusting Jesus. I have found to be true throughout the centuries that, *"The things which are impossible with men are possible with God"* (Luke 18:27).

I believe what we are to do with the impossible situations of life can be summed up in the words of Jesus, recorded for us in Matthew's Gospel. Jesus says, concerning this lad's lunch, *"Bring them hither to me"* (Matthew 14:18).

He doesn't give us a magic formula to solve our problems on our own. He doesn't specialize in the abracadabras of life, a rabbit foot in your pocket, or a dime tied around your ankle. Instead, He gives us Himself and invites us to cast our cares on Him. The apostle Peter stated:

"Casting all your care upon him; for he careth for you" (1 Peter 5:7).

Some people "drown their sorrows" in alcohol when they encounter difficulties in their life. Some people chain-smoke to "calm their nerves." Others, when things are not going well head to the refrigerator for, "another full course comfort meal."

God has better ideas. Instead of drowning in your sorrows, cast all your cares on Him. The Greek word for "cast" means to fling, toss, or to hurl in a sudden motion. In other words, "Let Jesus Have It."

Now first, think about the ways the disciples "responded" over the seeming impossibility of what they faced. See if you ever would have "responded" in the same manner. Let's take a microscopic view of what Jesus experienced.

I. The Testing of their Faith:

"And when it was evening, his disciples came to him, saying, This is a desert place, and the time is now past; send the multitude away, that they may go into the villages, and buy themselves victuals. But Jesus said unto them, They need not depart; give ye them to eat" (Matthew 14:15-16).

Theologians suggest that it was Philip who made this statement on behalf of the disciples. They focused more on the quantity of the crowd; rather than the quality of Jesus abilities. Philip arrived at the pragmatic conclusion that feeding five thousand people couldn't be done financially.

It would take more than two hundred denarii which was equivalent of eight to nine months wages, which only amounted to $12,000.00 in our today's value.

Let us not be so critical of Philips carnal ideology. We have experienced this type of situation before in our lives. Listen! Your mailbox is probably similar to mine. Sometimes there are more bills than paycheck. And your American Express now turns into American depressed! But, somewhere between your faith and your fatigue; Jesus made a way out of no way.

Philip declared they just didn't have the money to do what Jesus was suggesting. And even if they did, Bethsaida was a small town upon a hill, who would only have limited goods. There weren't enough stores and markets to buy the needed goods. They would have to travel out of town to get the needed supplies or have the supplies shipped to its destination. "Look at Jesus," He's testing their faith. The disciples encouraged Jesus to give the benediction, and send the people away.

These disciples have tarried with Jesus for three years, and it seems now they have abandoned their faith. The Kingdom of God as his disciples must remember to keep the faith in every crisis. Here's the remedy, "Let Jesus Have It." That's faith!

Faith is like a vending machine. When you approach that vending machine, insert your currency and select your desired item. You expect to receive what you purchased. This is what I call undoubting faith. This type of faith is what the Lord desires for His saints. No matter the circumstances one may face in life. He'll bring you through it.

II. The Tangible Fragmentation:

"There is a lad here, which have five barley loaves, and two small fishes: but what are they among so many?" (John 6:9).

They despaired over the provisions. All they had was the lunch that a little boy brought. It was nothing more than a "Kids Happy Meal."

My homiletical imagination forces me to believe that this little boy overheard the critical problem at hand, and volunteered to give up his lunch for the cause to help the vulnerable multitude.

It was enough perhaps to satisfy the hunger of a little boy, but certainly not enough to feed a multitude of thousands of people. It wasn't just five loaves and two fish, but John tells us, it was five "barley" loaves and two "small" fish. Barley loaves were pretty poor things to offer to people. Barley was cheap, and was usually reserved only as animal feed. The word John used to describe the fish is one that refers to a tiny sort of fish that you eat whole bones and all, much like modern day sardines.

As a result, the disciples clearly didn't want anything to do with this problem. To be realistic on a purely human level, who could have blamed them? The disciples were simply utilizing carnal common sense. They minimized this situation as humanly impossible to achieve.

Jesus says, "Bring them to me." In other words, put the little boys lunch in His hands, and give Him something to work with.

God is able to use the little things in life to make a big difference. He used a baby's cry to speak to Abraham. He used Moses rod to part the Red Sea. He used a stone and slingshot to remove Goliath. God can utilize small objects to remove large obstacles standing in our way. This two piece fish dinner wasn't too small for Jesus to use. It was more than enough!

Jesus ordered His disciples to make multitudes sit down. Mark tells us that they sat in ranks, in hundreds and fifties (Mark 6:40). Jesus made the people seat themselves into organized groups to get their food before He fed them. Perhaps, He wanted them to be able to enjoy fellowship as they ate. And able to communicate together concerning the miracle they were about to witness.

He took the five loaves and the two fish, and looking up to heaven, He blessed them. He took the time to give thanks to God, and to acknowledge Him for His provision. He took the time to worship His Father over the urgency of the need. He took time to Praise Him who integrated Himself into eternity pass, present and future.

He divided it up and distributed it through His disciples. They were the very ones who were complaining that all this was impossible, and no doubt, they were still thinking it was humanly impossible as they began to distribute the food. Jesus could have distributed it all Himself, and denied them the privilege of being involved in a notable miracle. Instead, He took the time to include them and use them.

This reminds us of the principle that once we bring our resources to Jesus, we must wait on His timing. Things might happen immediately after we turn things over to Him or they might not. They might be solved by Him the way we expect or they might not. It's all up to Him! When it seems as if He's delaying, who's to say that it's not because it was in His predestined will to accomplish several other things first. Things that were put on hold until we finally turned our resources over to Him.

Chapter 4

⌐₁₁

The Price Is Right

(Isaiah 53:1-5 KJV)

Who hath believed our report? and to whom is the arm of the LORD revealed? For he shall grow up before him as a tender plant, and as a root out of a dry ground: he hath no form nor comeliness; and when we shall see him, there is no beauty that we should desire him. He is despised and rejected of men; a man of sorrows, and acquainted with grief: and we hid as it were our faces from him; he was despised, and we esteemed him not. Surely he hath borne our griefs, and carried our sorrows: yet we did esteem him stricken, smitten of God, and afflicted. But he was wounded for our transgressions, he was bruised for our iniquities: the chastisement of our peace was upon him; and with his stripes we are healed.

The Price Is Right is an American game show centered on the pricing of merchandise to win cash and prizes. The current version of the show premiered on September 4, 1972 on CBS and was hosted by Bob Barker until his retirement on June 15, 2007. Drew Carey succeeded Barker at the beginning of Season 36 on October 15, 2007. *TV Guide* named *The Price Is Right* the greatest game show of all time. The show is well-known for its signature line of "Come on down! You're the next contestant on The Price Is Right."

There are varieties of games that are played on the Price Is Right! There's a game called:

The Check-Out, Cliff Hangers, Clock Game, Cover Up, Dice Game, Flip Flop, Hole In One, Line 'Em up, Make Your Move, Master Key, Temptation, and That's Too Much.

Without any demise and sanctioned in theological soundness, I venture to say that during the life and legacy of our Savior Jesus Christ, our Messiah, had an opportunity to either witness or experience many of these games, as if He was, "**The Next Contestant on The Price Is Right!**"

- **Line 'Em Up** – This is during the dispensation of God when He allowed thirty nine prophets to intercede before the coming of Jesus (1st Peter 1:10-12).
- **Temptation** – When He was tempted for forty days and forty nights by Satan (Luke 4:1-13).
- **That's Too Much** – When Judas with much indignation said, "Jesus didn't deserve the ointment that was place upon His body by Mary" (John 12:1-8).
- **Flip Flop** – When Peter was told by Jesus, that he would deny Him several times, and the cock will crow and remind him of his conviction (Mark 14:66-72).
- **Make Your Move** – This happened when Jesus told Judas, "Whatever you are going to do; do it quickly" (John 13:27).
- **Cliff Hangers** – When His enemies tried to apprehend him on edge of a cliff and He walked straight through the crowd (Luke 4:30).
- **Clock Game** – When He before his crucifixion said, "the hour has come that the Son of man must be betrayed" (John 12:23).
- **Hole In One** – When they lift up the cross and placed it in a hole to stabilize it with Jesus attached to it (John 12:32).
- **Dice Game** – When the soldiers gamble for Jesus garment at the foot of the cross (Mark 15:24).

- **Cover Up** – When it was told to the centurion soldier after Jesus resurrection to tell whoever asked where He is, tell them that "His disciples stole the body from the grave" (Matthew 28:12-13).
- **Master Key** – Jesus said to us that He has the keys of Hell and Death (Revelation 1:18).
- **Check-Out** – When He took a cloud and left the scene after his resurrection (Acts 1:9).

There was another game that had to be played and that's, "Die and get up again." The only contestant who has experienced this game and won is "Jesus." Notice the drastic episode Jesus had to endure. He was wounded, bruised, chastised, and striped!

There are four different injuries noted in verse five. He was wounded, bruised, chastised, and stripped.

The Lord suffered four different injuries on the cross. His feet and hands were pierced by nails. His brow was pierced by a crown of thorns. His side, and under His heart was pierced by a Roman spear.

He became what we are in order to redeem us from what we've become. Sin demanded a blood sacrifice! But a sheep had not committed the offence. So, in order to pay for the sins of the world; a human would have to die. There was only one problem. There had never been a sinless human. But now we see Him wounded in His hands, His heels, His head, and His heart.

I. His hands were Wounded for Our Transgressions:

Think about these hands that suffered the nails. They had cast the stars out into the universe. They had hung the moons and the planets in orbit, like hanging decorative balls on a Christmas tree. They had formed man out of the dust of the ground; like a potter forming clay. Those hands had taken the tip of the finger, and wrote the Ten Commandments on tablets of stone, as easy as you would write on a piece of paper.

They had been stretched out to receive the wounds that would pay for our sins. His hands were wounded for our transgressions. We have touched things that we shouldn't have touched, and handled things that we shouldn't have handled.

When you have a hard time with sin, and you want to do what you know that you shouldn't do, think about that precious hand being stretched out on that hard wooden cross.

I want you to realize that those wounds in His hands were just as much for you on that day, as they were for Thomas the doubting disciple.

As the hammer came down on the nails, I can't help but to think that He was thinking my name in His mind, and your name with every stroke on the nails.

II. His heels were bruised for Our Iniquities:

Let us take a moment and reflect about the feet of the Lord Jesus Christ. These feet stepped out into the vastness of nothing, and created everything. These feet stepped out of the portals of Heaven, and into the womb of a virgin. These feet walked on the water while it was raging beneath Him. These feet bore the burden of walking the cross up to Calvary's Hill. These feet were then bruised for our iniquities on that cross. But one day these feet will stand on the Mount of Olives, as Jesus assumes His throne, as the King of kings and the Lord of lords!

Here is the promise of the Redeemer. Just as Adam became sin to redeem his bride. So would Jesus Christ, become sin in order to redeem His bride, and all that would follow Him.

On the cross of Calvary, the spike was placed in the only part of the foot, which would both hold the weight of a man, and also would not break a bone. That place is the joint; where the heel meets the rest of the foot. The

Lords heel was bruised, but Satan's head was crushed. Satan didn't realize that he was nailing his own head to the cross.

He was wounded in His heel, because we went into places that we had no business stepping into. It breaks my heart to realize that it was the places that I've gone in my life that caused the Lord to suffer the bruises to those beautiful feet.

III. His head was chastised for Our Peace:

The head is arguably the most important extremity of the body. It holds the eyes by which we see. The ears by which we hear; the nose, by which we breathe, and the mouth by which we eat and drink. It also holds the brain, which is the abode of the mind, and the processing place for the soul.

When you think about His head being chastised, how they dressed Him out in Purple, blind folded Him, put a reed in His hand, then took it out of His hand and beat Him in the head with it until He suffered a literal concussion! Remember, He had you and me in mind on that day.

Think about the fact, that with His mouth, He spoke the creation into existence. With his eyes, He sees our needs before we have a problem. With His ears, He hears our prayers before we ever pray them while listening at the same time to our hurts, our fears, our praises, and our songs. It is this head, that we, the blood washed, redeemed saints of God, will one day crown as King of kings and Lord of lords, and His head was chastised for our peace!

IV. He opened not His Mouth:

He could have called the angels to avenge Him, but He opened not His mouth. He could have called fire down from heaven, but He opened not His mouth. He could have told the ground to open up and devour them, but He opened not His mouth.

You see! His head was chastened for the things that we thought, and the things that we heard, and the things that we saw, and tasted. That's what He was being chastened for.

He was crowned, by a thorny crown, to gain our peace with God. One day, we'll repay the favor, when we take the crowns given to us at the judgment seat and crown Him King with a golden crown!

We have seen how His hands were wounded for our transgressions, and how His heels were bruised for our iniquities, and how His head was chastised for our peace.

V. His Heart was striped for our Healing:

We needed healing because, without Christ, we are sick, "*But when Jesus heard that, he said unto them, They that be whole need not a physician, but they that are sick*" (Matthew 9:12).

You see, we are like the blind man who cannot see what is ahead of Him, like the crippled man who is crooked and unable to stand on His own, like the leper that is sick from the inside out and like the children of Israel, bitten by fiery serpents, sick from a snake bite. The only antidote is made from the very same poison that has made you sick.

That is why Jesus had to drink the cup of sin in the garden of Gethsemane, and that is why the bible says, "*For he hath made him to be sin for us, who knew no sin; that we might be made the righteousness of God in him*" (2 Corinthians 5:21).

He was scourged at the whipping post by pilot, until you could see the inner parts of the muscle torn, and the ligaments and even some of the organs were visible to the world.

Then, after that, He carried a heavy wooden cross up to the top of a hill and laid Himself down on His own free will. After the centurion soldiers dropped the cross into the hole ripping His flesh, after God had turned the sky black and poured out His wrath upon sin, after He commended His Spirit into the hands of the Father and gave up the Ghost, after all this, they had one more stripe to lay upon Him.

"But one of the soldiers with a spear pierced his side, and forthwith came there out blood and water" (John 19:34).

Now, this was supernatural in nature, as well as natural. The blood was the agent to which salvation would be given, and the living water. The Holy Spirit would be the agent whereby salvation would be kept.

There is a medical condition that can help to explain this as well. When the heart suffers great trauma, the sack around the heart will fill with a watery fluid. Jesus, did not die of a scourging, or a Roman cross, or of any other earthly reason, He died of a broken heart, which burst forth the cleansing blood, and the living water of the Holy Spirit.

He loved us enough that He gave his cheek to the smiters, and opened not His mouth to the accusers. This should cause us to be bold in our service to Him, and never let us forget what our salvation cost. It may have been free to us, but it was certainly not cheap.

Remember what Jesus suffered, "**The Price was Right**."

Chapter 5

⌒✐⌒

What Was In the Cup?

(Matthew 26:38-44 KJV)

*Then saith he unto them, My soul is exceeding sorrowful,
even unto death: tarry ye here, and watch with me. And he
went a little farther, and fell on his face, and prayed, saying,
O my Father, if it be possible, let this cup pass from me:
nevertheless not as I will, but as thou wilt. And he cometh
unto the disciples, and findeth them asleep, and saith unto
Peter, What, could ye not watch with me one hour? Watch
and pray, that ye enter not into temptation: the spirit indeed
is willing, but the flesh is weak. He went away again the
second time, and prayed, saying, O my Father, if this cup may
not pass away from me, except I drink it, thy will be done.
And he came and found them asleep again: for their eyes were
heavy. And he left them, and went away again, and prayed
the third time, saying the same words.*

Located in the beautiful city of Jerusalem on the eastern side is
the Mount of Olives. On the western side is a garden called
Gethsemane. This is the geographical location that Jesus used as
His personal prayer closet.

When Jesus entered the garden of Gethsemane with His Inner Circle,
it would become a night of agony, agitation and aggression. While in the
garden Peter, James and John because of human frailty, showed Jesus no

companionship. They slept on Jesus! This continued till Judas arrived to betray Jesus to the chief priests and scribes, for less than twenty dollars.

There will be times when we must enter our **"Garden of Gethsemane."** There will be times of distress, sorrow, loneliness, but such times can also be a time of comfort and strength provided we spend them in prayer, and be willing to accept the Father's will.

Jesus found prayer to be the key for turning a garden of suffering into a garden of strength. This night was no ordinary night for our Savior. He had shared His last meal with His disciples. He had spoken volumes concerning his crucifixion, and He had motivated Judas to move quickly, so that the scriptures might be fulfilled.

"Yea, mine own familiar friend, in whom I trusted, which did eat of my bread, hath lifted up his heel against me" (Psalms 41:9).

In this Garden Jesus requested of His Father, " *O my Father, if this cup may not pass away from me, except I drink it, thy will be done"* (Matthew 26:42).

I. The Pollution of Sin was in that Cup:

The Pollution of sin was in Gethsemane's cup. It was Jesus who had to conquer sin, and concluded His Redemptive work to cleanse us of our sins, by way of His death. In the Garden of Gethsemane Jesus ordered Satan's coffin, and at Calvary after His resurrection, Jesus put a nail in it!

Jesus was tempted in all points as we are, yet He was without sin.

"For we have not an high priest which cannot be touched with the feeling of our infirmities; but was in all points tempted like as we are, yet without sin" (Hebrews 4:15).

God made Him, Jesus, to be sin for us (2 Corinthians 5:21). Gethsemane's cup was full of my sins and your sins. The sins of the every vile thoughts and wicked deeds were in that cup.

Jesus decided to drink of that cup while in the garden. It was not a coincidence that Christ would choose to bring salvation to mankind in a garden. Let's investigate and contrast Adams Garden of Eden, and Jesus' Garden of Gethsemane.

In Eden Adam and Eve were conversing with the ruler of darkness	In Gethsemane Christ was conversing with the Father of Lights
In Eden Adam and Eve sinned	In Gethsemane Christ agonized over the suffering for that sin
In Eden Adam and Eve fell before Satan	In Gethsemane Christ fell before His Father
In Eden the race that was to come from Adam was lost	In Gethsemane the race which would come from Christ was found
In Eden Adam took the forbidden fruit from Eve	In Gethsemane Christ took the forbidden cup of suffering from the Father
In Eden Adam hid himself from the face of God	In Gethsemane Christ kneeled Himself before the presence of God
In Eden the sword was drawn to block Adam from the Tree of Life	In Gethsemane the sword was sheathed to open the way to the Tree of Life in Christ
In Eden a Tree was rooted in Delight	In Gethsemane a Tree was rooted in Misery and Suffering

II. Punishment of Sin was in that Cup:

It was because of the ingredients of the "cup" which He had to drink, if sinners were to be saved (Matthew 26:39).

Jesus wasn't talking about a literal cup, like one you could hold in your hand. He was using a figure of speech meaning, "to experience something fully." Meaning "to take something into one's being."

Atheism and Hedonism was in that cup, idolatry was in that cup, profanity and disobedience were in that cup, and murder was in that cup. Adultery was also in that cup along with hatred and gossip. Just to name a few! They were all in Gethsemane's cup.

The "cup" was a metaphor used in reference to the judgment of God which was to fall on the sinless Saviour as He bore our sins (Isaiah 53:6); as He took away our sins (John 1:29); as He became sin for us (2 Corinthians 5:21). As the Saviour anticipated this and the rejection He would experience (Matthew 27:46), He was overcome with the anguish of it.

Before the world was created, Jesus had agreed to drink this cup to save the ones He loves. He would not just take a sip of it, but would drink to the bottom of the cup, until there was nothing left. How His spirit must have assailed Him as our Lord, as fully human as He was fully God, waiting to drink this cup for our impurities.

When God handed the cup to Jesus; He drank it all, sparing all of us!

- **He entered the Garden as Lord, He left as a Lamb.**
- **He entered the Garden in Honor, He left in humiliation.**
- **He entered the Garden with His friends, He left friendless.**
- **He entered the Garden sinless; He left as a sin-offering.**
- **He entered the Garden free, He left bound.**
- **He entered the Garden in authority, He left in agony.**

If He had not said, "Thy will be done in the Garden", He would have been unable to say, "It is finished" at Calvary.

Let's rejoice! Be thankful that Christ drank the cup to the bottom. Be thankful, knowing that all of eternity would not be enough time for you to drink that cup. Jesus' sacrifice was so great, so complete, that what He drank in several hours, you could not drink if you had the rest of time to do so. Look not to the time of His suffering, but to the intensity.

Praise Him! Rest in Him and in His infinite, complete, awesome love. Rejoice that your cup is empty, consumed in the greatest act of love the world will ever experience.

Chapter 6

⁓

Are We There Yet?

(Exodus 13:17-22 KJV)

And it came to pass, when Pharaoh had let the people go, that God led them not through the way of the land of the Philistines, although that was near; for God said, Lest peradventure the people repent when they see war, and they return to Egypt: But God led the people about, through the way of the wilderness of the Red sea: and the children of Israel went up harnessed out of the land of Egypt. And Moses took the bones of Joseph with him: for he had straitly sworn the children of Israel, saying, God will surely visit you; and ye shall carry up my bones away hence with you. And they took their journey from Succoth, and encamped in Etham, in the edge of the wilderness. And the LORD went before them by day in a pillar of a cloud, to lead them the way; and by night in a pillar of fire, to give them light; to go by day and night: He took not away the pillar of the cloud by day, nor the pillar of fire by night, from before the people.

When you are on a journey with small children; there's one question you will sooner or later have to face. The kids definitely will ask it. They will ask it even though you warn them you never want to hear it again. They will ask it as if they had a judicial legal obligation to do it. It will irritate you like fingernails scraping up against blackboard. The inquisitive question will be, "Daddy, are we there yet?" "Mother, are we there yet?" "Papa, are we there yet?" Hopefully, I'm not the only one who has been asked this inquisitive question, "Are we there yet?"

In the tenor and the tone of the text, God was about to lead Israel out of Egyptian captivity. There was a well traveled highway, a major trade-route called the Via Maris that ran straight from Egypt to Palestine. It was heavily guarded by Egyptian forts to protect against any possible invading armies. It ran through Philistine territory. You could call it the, "Philistine Inter-State."

It would have taken Israel about ten days to make the journey. This might sound simple enough! Yet, God had a detour in mind. He took Israel the long way around. God led them in the direction of the Red Sea instead which at first glance seemed like a dead end road.

God often does not lead us along the shortest route in this life in which we live. If you permit the Lord to direct your steps, expect to be led occasionally on paths that may seem unnecessarily long and indirect. It's imperative to remind yourself that God knows what He's doing, and He isn't in a hurry.

On the day of the Exodus, the whole nation gathered. This is the day they've waited for after 400 years of bondage. They are setting out on their exciting journey to the promise land. The Israelites had-no maps, no GPS, no Global Positioning Satellite to guide them. They've got something much better! They have a pillar of cloud by day, and a pillar of fire by night to usher them to the promise land.

God ushered them with His presence. What else did they have going for them? Well, they had the reminder of God's promises in the bones of Joseph. There they are looking at Joseph bones in his coffin. They are remembering promises that had been made hundreds of years ago to their ancestors, long before Joseph, remembering that God had amazingly fulfilled His promises.

After four hundred years, surely there would have been some in Israel who doubted whether God was going to fulfill His promises. But just in case any doubter would be told, "Look at the box, look at the box, Joseph's bones are in that box, just like he said he would be, just like he said God would do; God is taking us out of Egypt."

God is ushering them out of Egypt, across the Red Sea, through the wilderness and into their final destination the promise land. They are already in battle formation. The men are in front in case of an ambush, and in the rear, the more vulnerable stand with weakness in their knees. The pillar of fire and cloud starts to move, but it's going the wrong way! The Promised Land is north and God is going south. He's taking a big detour!

God's has his reasoning behind taking a detour. I imagine God said, "If they take the Philistine Interstate, take the easy way and then suddenly run headfirst into a major conflict, they might backslide, and return to Egypt." If life was too easy, if we never had a setback and had smooth sailings most of our lives, then when something ambushes us, like heart disease, we might not be prepared on how to handle the situation.

Remember as a kid learning to ride a bike? At first your dad ran behind you holding up the bicycle. Then he decided to let you go. You fell down more than a few times, but you got back up because you enjoyed the ride. God wants us to grow up, and learn to ride the obstacles of life that knock us down. But because we enjoy the ride, when we fall, we get right back up again all in due time. He never gives us more than we can handle until we're ready for it. The question still arise "Are we there yet?"

God led Israel on a roundabout way through the desert toward the Red Sea. He even told Israel to reverse course, and make camp on a dead end road up against the Red Sea. It led Pharaoh to think, "They're lost and confused. I'll run them down and bring them back to Egypt again."

Egypt represents, **Satan's kingdom of darkness**. The taskmasters represent the **fallen angels** and **demons**. Pharaoh represents **Satan himself** and of course, the Israelite represents **God's spirit children** who are in bondage to sin all over the Earth.

The name "Pharaoh" means "sun" or "his nakedness." Pharaoh's effects and dominance in the affairs of our life scorches and burns us in the wrong way. He strips us bare, leaving us destitute, naked, exposed and defeated.

He reduces us to slaves in a slime pit! God's will is that we are in His Son (Jesus Christ) and personally know the truth and power of being covered and clothed by His precious blood.

God said, "I will use Pharaoh and his army to put my Glory on display before all Egypt!" Pharaoh took the bait and came charging like killer bees behind God's children

Israel chickened out and complained, "God weren't the cemeteries big enough in Egypt that you took us into the desert to die? We would've been better off back in slavery!" God said, "You just wait and see!" The problem with us is. When God moved on our behalf, we refuse to let Him work it out! There's too much complaining and not enough Hallelujah! "Are we there yet?"

Do you know that God specializes in ushering?

Often times, we do not know or forget from whence comes ushering. God was the very first usher. He ushered in day and light (Genesis 1:3-4) and ushered man into the Garden of Eden (Genesis 2:15).

Ushers or forerunners are depicted throughout the Bible. Abraham ushered faithfulness into the world (Genesis 22). Moses ushered the children of Israel out of the land of Egypt (Exodus 15). Joshua his successor ushered them into the promise land (Joshua 1).

God ushered Himself into Mary. The Star of Bethlehem ushered the wise men of the east to the place where Christ ushered Himself into a manger. John the Baptist, forerunner of Christ, ushered the coming of Christ, and prepared the way. He was the voice crying in the wilderness (John 1:6-13).

The pillar of cloud and fire moved between the Egyptian army and Israel like a shield. God sent a powerful east wind that pushed the seawater back which opened a land bridge to safety. Families ran forward as babies cried, children left footprints in the sand, cattle and sheep bleated, and the whole congregation got through to the other side.

When the Egyptians tried to follow, the wheels of their chariots stuck in the mud. Seaweed wrapped around their axles like hands holding them back. Then with a roar like Niagara Falls the wall of water collapsed over them, and not one of Pharaohs' army men survived. Israel stood marveled while watching God's power and glory.

I can hear someone in the crowd saying, "We made it" and asked Moses, "So where do we go from here?" Throughout the bible God sums it up in two words, if you want to know where we're going "Follow me!"

God ushered them through the wilderness by means of the pillar of cloud by day and fire by night. That fire by night should remind you of Moses at the burning bush that was not consumed when the Angel of the Lord spoke out the flames. Think of Mt Sinai it was covered with cloud, smoke, lightning and fire. The awesome presence of God!

It was there upon Mount Sinai, where God gave the Ten Commandments. His written word as a spiritual road guide for his people, and today we have the bible. What's more important we have the Holy Spirit, who sets our heart on fire like he did the disciples at Pentecost.

Before you begin your journey today; I encourage you to take Jesus with you. You too will face unexpected "detours" in your life journey and you will never be more aware of how close you can get to Christ in those moments. He may take you on a roundabout way. You might ask more than once, "Are we there yet?" We're close! We're closer than we've ever been before. Soon and very soon, he will get us home to the Promised Land. Amen!

Chapter 7

✧

Is the Lord among Us or Not?

(Exodus 17:7-8 KJV)

And he called the name of the place Massah, and Meribah, because of the chiding of the children of Israel, and because they tempted the LORD, saying, Is the LORD among us, or not? Then came Amalek, and fought with Israel in Rephidim.

Have you ever wondered if God is real? Have you ever thought to yourself, "What if there is no God after all?"

The question is often asked in the midst of crisis or discouragement, "Is the Lord among us or not?" In the book of Exodus the Israelites ask the very question. After their escape from Egypt and God's destruction of the Egyptian army in the Red Sea, Moses led the people into the desert on their way to the Promised Land.

But immediately they ran into trouble:

"So Moses brought Israel from the Red sea, and they went out into the wilderness of Shur; and they went three days in the wilderness, and found no water. And when they came to Marah, they could not drink of the waters of Marah, for they were bitter: therefore the name of it was called Marah" (Exodus 15:22-23).

"And they took their journey from Elim, and all the congregation of the children of Israel came unto the wilderness of Sin, which is between Elim and

Sinai, on the fifteenth day of the second month after their departing out of the land of Egypt. And the whole congregation of the children of Israel murmured against Moses and Aaron in the wilderness:" (Exodus 16:1-2).

"And all the congregation of the children of Israel journeyed from the wilderness of Sin, after their journeys, according to the commandment of the LORD, and pitched in Rephidim: and there was no water for the people to drink. And the people thirsted there for water; and the people murmured against Moses, and said, Wherefore is this that thou hast brought us up out of Egypt, to kill us and our children and our cattle with thirst?" (Exodus 17:1, 3).

But the text says, *"And he called the name of the place Massah, and Meribah, because of the chiding of the children of Israel, and because they tempted the LORD, saying, Is the LORD among us, or not?"* (Exodus 17:7).

When it ain't one thing, it's another!

While at Rephidim the enemy struck them unannounced. The Amalekites came and attacked the Israelites while they were empty handed (Exodus 17:8).

What is the meaning of Rephidim?

"Rephidim" means "rests" (plural). One cannot take this too far but it does at least raise the thought that we are often most vulnerable when everything seems calm and restful. The point is that our enemy never sleeps and we too must remain ever vigilant and on guard even when we "rest."

The Amalekites attacked from the rear, picking off the stragglers. You might remember that the Amalekites are the descendants of Abraham's great great grandson Amalek. Amalek, the son of Eliphaz is the grandson

son of Esau which is Eliphaz father. The Israelites are the descendants of Jacob the brother of Esau who are the sons of Isaac who father is Abraham, which makes the Amalekites, and the Israelites first cousins. "These are relatives who refuse to get along."

The Amalekites always tried to attack the physical as well as the spiritual mobility of Israel. Whenever the children of "God" spiritual mobility is attacked, those who have attacked you will have control over your spiritual outcome if you allow them to!

Here's what I'm trying to say:

The way you think will determine the way you feel; the way you feel will Influence the way you act.

Regardless of how the Amalekites treated the Israelites! The Amalekites never prevailed. God always in their darkest hour turned their situation into sunshine.

The animosity between these two tribes was already hundreds of years old and would continue for at least another 1500 years down to the birth of Christ when Herod, a descendant of Esau's grandson Amalek, would attempt to kill Jesus Christ. Treachery ran in the Amalekites family!

In Jewish tradition, the Amalekites became the symbol of evil incarnate:

This was not just a tribal battle. This was an eruption of a cosmic battle between God and Satan. And the battlefield was the people of God. Perhaps, this attack by the Amalekites was an attack against the Israelites because of their ungratefulness toward the Lord. The Israelites were already sinful in their nature, and God was offended because of their track record.

The same is true today!

We too often treat the temptation to sin and even sin itself in our lives as little matters, sometimes even funny matters. Violence, immorality, vengeance, profanity, greed, and sin have become subjects of entertainment, presented in ways to make us laugh.

We hold the burning embers of lust, anger or bitterness to our chests as if they will not burn us. We forget the clear warning of God, *"abstain from fleshly lusts, which war against the soul"* (1 Peter 2:11).

Satan was out to destroy the people of God then and he is still at it. While Apostle Peter was taking communion in that first Lord's Supper, even in that great spiritual experience, Jesus looked at him and said, *"Simon, Simon, Satan has a desire (has asked) to sift you as wheat"* (Luke 22:31).

Notice what Moses instructed:

(Exodus 17:8-10 KJV)

Then came Amalek, and fought with Israel in Rephidim. And Moses said unto Joshua, Choose us out men, and go out, fight with Amalek: to morrow I will stand on the top of the hill with the rod of God in mine hand. So Joshua did as Moses had said to him, and fought with Amalek: and Moses, Aaron, and Hur went up to the top of the hill.

The focus of the story is not on Joshua on the battlefield, but on Moses who is on the mountain standing with his hands lifted to God, and Joshua is winning the battle against the Amalekites.

When Moses' hands are raised with the staff, Joshua is winning battle. In battle the raising of hands symbolize praying and giving reverence to

God. When Moses' hands are lowered with the staff, Joshua is losing battle. The specific mention of the "staff of God" symbolizes God's presence and power.

- Exodus 4:2-4 - this staff is the one God turned into a snake to convince Moses originally.
- Exodus 4:17-20 - this is the staff God told him to take to Egypt, to perform the miracles of the plagues. It is here first that it was called "the staff of God."
- Exodus (see chapters 7-12) - It was this staff that the plagues were initiated.
- Exodus 14:16 - It was this staff that parted the Red Sea.

Moses is praying, which is the highest expression of confidence in God, and Joshua is winning the battle. God clearly ordained prayer as the primary means by which the battle would be won. Whenever, Moses' arms would get tired, he dropped his hands. So the battle would then turn against Joshua.

What was God doing in this?

I think it dramatically demonstrates that the battle belonged to the Lord, not even to mighty Moses. Moses grew so tried in prayer that Aaron and Hur had to get him a chair, and sit him down, and hold his hands up.

- The chair represented the authority of his Position.
- The holding up of his hands represents the accountability of his Position.

We must realize that God is constantly with us! Remember the question? "Is the Lord with us or not?"

God has answered it in a dramatic fashion:

(Exodus 17:14-16 KJV)

And the LORD said unto Moses, Write this for a memorial in a book, and rehearse it in the ears of Joshua: for I will utterly put out the remembrance of Amalek from under heaven. And Moses built an altar, and called the name of it Jehovahnissi: For he said, Because the LORD hath sworn that the LORD will have war with Amalek from generation to generation.

And the name he gave the memorial also speaks to the truth that God was the source of the victory over evil – "The Lord is my Banner." "Jehovah Nissi."

The American flag is the banner of the United States of America and stands for the presence and power of the USA, so this banner symbolized the real power behind the victory that day because of the Lord.

In conclusion, I would like to ask a question. Will you help lift up holy hands in prayer and not let them down? We need some Aarons and Hurs to help hold our hands up and to keep us praying.

We need each other, to hold each other accountable for praying, and leading our families in prayer. Our main objective should include praying for our mission as a church, and for praying for the Kingdom of God. "Is the Lord among Us or Not?" The answer is definitely!

Chapter 8

～

What Happened To The Noise?

(Psalms 100:1-5 KJV)

Make a joyful noise unto the LORD, all ye lands. Serve the LORD with gladness: come before his presence with singing. Know ye that the LORD he is God: it is he that hath made us, and not we ourselves; we are his people, and the sheep of his pasture. Enter into his gates with thanksgiving, and into his courts with praise: be thankful unto him, and bless his name. For the LORD is good; his mercy is everlasting; and his truth endureth to all generations.

In our traditional congregational setting many people bring all kinds of things to church that cause extremely loud noises. I've noticed some bring snacks, candy, cell phones, iPods, and toys to entertain the kids. Any noise that replaces the noise of worship should be exempt from the sanctuary entirely.

Psalm 100 is a Psalm of the future millennial kingdom; it describes what worship will be like in the day when the Lord Jesus Christ reigns in glory, and power upon the earth. However, we are not in that glorious day at the present, but we are in the royal priesthood of God and we are commanded to gather ourselves together and worship Him in His church.

Not forsaking the assembling of ourselves together, as the manner of some is; but exhorting one another: and so much the more, as ye see the day approaching (Hebrews 10:25).

It is too bad that real worship is fast becoming a massive case of amnesia in America. In fact, many preposterous things are going on under the title of "Worship."

Illustration:

In one church, the congregation gathers never speaking to one another waiting for the spiritual one to come into the high pulpit and read to them from the mystifying book. In another building across town, the Sunday morning version of Soul Train and BET, is taking place. The hype man introduces the preacher, singers, and the Lord of entertainment is worshipped. In another place, two groups meet in one room. They habitually gather each week for this day of formal procedure, but the strife between the two factions does not allow room for God or his worship.

God want us to worship him when we gather. What we do in the sanctuary should be for his honor and glory. Therefore, we need to examine the scriptures and see what God demands.

I. Make a Joyful Noise:

Make a joyful noise! Our expectation should set the atmosphere for authentic worship. There's no melodic reason to sing like Mariah Carey or Tina Turner in order to worship God. God is not so much interested in our tone and pitch as he is in our heart-felt expression.

When children sing "Yes Jesus loves me" That is worship. When some of you, turn loose on your favorite hymn, singing to God from the bottom of your heart. That is real worship!

We must personally decree worship in every area of opportunity in our lives. We must continue to declare the victory over the enemy, on behalf of our relationship and righteousness as we worship our God!

God wants the world to hear the joy of his people. Worship should not be a spectator sport. It is not something you sit and watch. It is something you do. It is you expressing your love for God.

II. Serve Him with Gladness: (Singing)

There are 165 references in the Bible to singing. God wants us to sing praises unto Him. The songs we sing on Sunday morning are not just a warm up for the preached word. It is acknowledging that He is God and that we are his creatures. So, when singing time extends its opportunity to praise Him, sing loud! "Express yourself before you wreck yourself!"

We have some people who would say, "Wait one minute, I'm not the emotional type. I just don't get into the emotional scene." But what about seeing you at a football game?" Were you screaming and yelling? Were you jumping up and down? Were you waving your hands in the air? Then surprisingly later after the game, you talked about it for hours. Therefore, it seemed like you were the emotional type. If you are fired up at a football game, you should be even more fired up to praise God in the sanctuary.

III. Be Thankful unto Him:

When we come into His presence, we need to come with thanksgiving on our lips and in our heart. The bible says, *"Death and life are in the power of the tongue: and they that love it shall eat the fruit thereof"* (Proverbs 18:21).

Your mouth puts a demand on what will come to you. We are guilty of being an ungrateful people, always complaining and moaning about how bad we have it. We should be thanking God for so many things. Thank God for health, salvation, friends, family, and freedom.

Worship begins by acknowledging God's place in your life. More importantly, you will worship the one who sits on the throne of your life. The one who lives for himself cannot worship. Those who do not recognize that they are the creatures and God is the creator cannot worship. The man who has refused the loving mercy of God cannot worship God.

For the Lord is Good, his mercy is everlasting; and his truth endureth to all generations (Psalms 100:5).

Jesus is God's ultimate expression of his Goodness and Mercy. Why? Because he died for us, so that we can have a marvelous relationship with God.

Chapter 9

༄

A Mother's Tears

(Proverbs 10:1 KJV)

The proverbs of Solomon. A wise son maketh a glad father:
but a foolish son is the heaviness of his mother.

It is good to commit to memory. Exactly who wrote the jewels of wisdom called proverbs? Since he wrote primarily to his son and young men, each son should consider his relationship to his parents. Not until he is a parent will he understand the joy and grief he can cause by his choices and actions. Let every young man consider his mother, his father, and His Heavenly Father above.

One of the most moving moments of life is to watch your mother cry. No matter how difficult life gets, mother will remind you every now and then, "Baby it's alright to cry, get it all out and you'll feel so much better."

Mother has many reasons to cry depending on the circumstances that she's facing. Sometimes she will disperse tears of joy, happiness, frustration, pain, perplexity, devotion, dependence and determination. It's very difficult at time to watch your mother cry, and don't understand why.

I'm reminded of a story of a little boy concerning his mother's tears:

"Why are you crying?" he asked his Mom. "Because I'm a mother," she told him. "I don't understand," he said. His mom just hugged him to her and said, "You never will."

Later the little boy asked his father why mother seemed to cry for no reason. "All mothers cry for no reason," was all his dad could say.

The little boy grew up and became a man, still wondering why mothers cry. One night, he had a dream. In his dream, he called God on the telephone and when God came to the phone the man asked, "God, why do mothers cry so easily?" God answered him, "My son, you see, when I made mothers, I knew they had to be special."

I made their shoulders strong enough to carry the weight of the world, yet gentle enough to give comfort. I gave them an inner strength to endure childbirth and the rejection that many times come from their children and mates. I gave them a hardiness that allows them to keep going when everyone else gives up, and to take care of their families through sickness and fatigue without complaining. I gave them the sensitivity to love their children under all circumstances, even when their child has hurt them very badly.

This same sensitivity helps them to make a child's boo-boo feel better and helps them share a teenager's anxieties and fears. I gave them a tear to shed. It's theirs, exclusively, to use whenever needed. It's their only weakness. It is a tear for mankind. (**Author Unknown**)

Every living soul, if your mother is living, you should to be grateful that God has allowed her life to roll on a little while longer. Let me hurriedly say, "It takes a woman to develop a child, but it takes a real mother to raise one."

There are three mothers I would like to investigate who have shed tears on behalf of their child or children.

I. For the child not born, "Hannah had a reason to cry"

a) Hannah (1st Samuel 1:1-10)

Hannah was barren and she desired of the Lord a man child. Hannah was ridiculed royally and despised by a woman named Peninnah, who was also married to her husband Elkanah, and each day this woman Peninnah would agitate Hannah to the point of exhaustion and tears. But! Hannah knew the remedy of getting her request through to God, by way of prayer. God blessed her womb to give birth to the man child Samuel, who became the judge over Israel. His mother Hannah prayer was answered.

Every mother should to be a praying woman like that of Hannah. And every child should thank God for a mother who is steadfast in prayer.

Furthermore, a good mother will teach her children how to pray and remind them, perhaps if they pray something is bound to happen. If their prayers are authentic, that specific prayer will soon bring about a change effective immediately.

II. For children at odds, "Rebekah had a reason to cry" (Esau / Jacob)

a) Rebekah (Genesis 25:21-23)

Rebekah had problems with at least two of her boys that were twins, and they were fighting within her womb before they were delivered. Rebekah had to consult the Lord about her child to get a better understanding of why they were acting the way they were, and God informed Rebekah that these boys would envy each other.

Job said, *"Man that is born of a woman is but a few days and full of trouble"* (Job 14:1).

When they became older, Rebekah had to send Jacob away. Esau had planned to take Jacob's life. Rebekah had to work it out, although she was part of the hostility. This happened after Jacob the trickster stole Esau's birthright from his blind father Isaac by pretending to be Esau.

It destroys a mother when she sees that her own children are confrontational with each other. I believe that Rebekah entered into her secret closet, beseeching God to work out the indifferences, as she shed tears on her children behalf. I'm a witness, that a mother can do more with tear drops, than the state can do with an electric chair!

Our mothers taught us many things about life in general:

- **My mother taught me Religion:**
  "You better pray that will come out of the carpet."
- **My mother taught me about Time Travel:**
  "If you don't straighten up, I'm going to knock you into the middle of next week!"
- **My mother taught me Logic:**
  "Because I said so, that's why."
- **My mother taught me Foresight:**
  "Make sure you wear clean underwear, in case you're in an accident."
- **My mother taught me Irony:**
  "Keep crying and I'll give you something to cry about."
- **My mother taught me about the science of Osmosis:**
  "Shut your mouth and eat your supper!"
- **My mother taught me about Stamina:**
  "You'll sit there till all that spinach is finished."
- **My mother taught me about Weather:**
  "It looks as if a tornado swept through your room."

- **My mother taught me about Behavior Modification:**
  "Stop acting like your father!"
- **My mother taught me about Anticipation:**
  "Just wait until we get home."
- **My mother taught me ESP:**
  "Put your sweater on; don't you think I know when you're cold?"
- **My mother taught me about Wisdom of Age:**
  "When you get to be my age, you will understand."

III. For the child that suffers, "Mary had a reason to cry"

a) Mary (John 19:26–27)

Mary, the good mother, grieves at the cross of her Son, because she can no longer care for him. Everything that a good mother would do, she's prevented from doing. Jesus is beaten and bloody, thorns are pressed into his brow and scalp. His skin is ripped apart in dozens of places and His face is covered with a grimy paste of dirt, blood, and sweat. Suppose you're the mother of Jesus who sees this. What would your heart cry out to do?

You would desire to get him down from that cross and lay him on something more convenient. You want to get fresh water and clean cloths, to gently wash away the filth and blood. You want to dress and bandage his wounds. That's the type of thing you've always done for your Son, but now! You are prevented from achieving this responsibility.

They won't let you near him, so Jesus suffers alone. And those clothes you made for him. Those clean, sturdy clothes of wool and linen yarn you'd spun and woven yourself. Have all been ripped off his body by the soldiers, even his undergarment!

This good man that you've raised and clothed is hanging there like a slice of beef, naked and bloody but alive. And everyone is watching. Many are laughing and mocking your Son. Oh, how you want to get him down and cover him up! A good and caring mother doesn't let her son run naked in the street. She doesn't let him hang naked from a cross either, but you can't do a thing to help him.

You can't even get him a cup of water when he says, "I'm thirsty." How many times must Mary have brought Jesus cups of cold water she'd drawn from the well in Nazareth?

How many times had he run into the house as a child, hot and tired from playing in the street, and she'd given him a cool cup of water? How many times had she taken water to Joseph and Jesus as they labored in the sun, thirsty and sweaty from cutting logs into boards, covered with sawdust, and given them a refreshing cup of water?

Now Jesus needs a cool cup of water more than he's ever needed it in his life. A good mother wants to give him one, but she can't. She can only grieve in gloom for him. She's met all these needs thousands of times before, but now she can't. She's helpless and sheds her tears.

The godly mother has many tears, but God keeps those tears in His bottle.

"Thou tellest my wanderings: put thou my tears into thy bottle: are they not in thy book? When I cry unto thee, then shall mine enemies turn back: this I know; for God is for me" (Psalm 56:8-9).

Thank God for, "A Mother's Tear."

Chapter 10

‿‿‿

Walk With Me Lord

(Genesis 5:22-24 KJV)

And Enoch walked with God after he begat Methuselah three hundred years, and begat sons and daughters: And all the days of Enoch were three hundred sixty and five years: And Enoch walked with God: and he was not; for God took him.

Genesis chapter five is like a cemetery, or it reads more like an obituary column. If and when you get the opportunity, read Genesis chapter five, verse five. *"And all of these days that Adam lived were nine hundred and thirty years,"* and notice the next phrase, *"and he died."* And then verse eight. *And all of the days of Seth were nine hundred and twelve years,"* but notice the refrain, *"and he died."* Now look at verse eleven. *"All of the days of Enos were nine hundred and five years and he died."* We could go on talking about death hall of fame, and he died and he died and he died and he died, it reads like an obituary column. But! There is one name that stands out, and it is the name of Enoch.

Notice in verse twenty one and see the change of pace, see the difference. *"And Enoch lived sixty and five years and begat Methuselah, and Enoch walked with God after he begat Methuselah three hundred years and begat sons and daughters and all of the days of Enoch were three hundred sixty and five years."* You would think it would say that he died but look, *"And Enoch walked with God and he was not for God took him."*

His whole life before this divine abduction is compared to our calendar which consists of three hundred and sixty five days, which indicates that we must walk with the Lord every day of the year.

I. Enoch's Relationship with God:

Enoch, the seventh generation from Adam, was a very special person, a man that followed his religion. Enoch had no Jack in a box religion. He walked by faith and not by feeling.

Enoch walked so closely with God in consistent fellowship that God took him to heaven without him ever experiencing death. He was God's first astronaut. Here is the creature, God's master piece in constant contact with our creator, dust with divinity, finite with the infinite.

Enoch made God's word and promises his rule and always glorified Him. God's word was the rule of his faith. All his actions were directed to the glory of God who, the Heavens declared his glory.

Enoch's spiritual communion and fellowship grew as the years evaporated. The fellowship that Enoch enjoyed with God was not an infrequent relationship. Where we just walk with Him whenever we need Him; and sit down when we are fifteen cents above bus fair. His relationship was a rather ongoing way of lifestyle. What a marvelous walk with the Lord, for three hundred years. His walk was not a dash, a soar, a dive, a sprint, but a steady and continuous walk.

It seems difficult for Christians today to walk with God for a single day. However, Enoch's heart was in harmony with God's will. There were others, who were dedicated to the cause of righteousness, and had fellowship with God and one another. But here is a man that had a continued walk with God and He took him.

II. Enoch's Requirement for God:

a) Enoch's Preaching:

In Enoch's generation there were many multitudes, a large majority of the people, who did not believe in God. They did not believe Noah, and they did not believe Enoch. The same is true of our generation, "I won't believe in God, until I see Him for myself."

Enoch didn't mince his words when he preached to an ungodly nation. You didn't have to wonder what message Enoch was trying to get across. When Enoch preached to an ungodly world he warned of the impending verdict and called for repentance.

What I like about Enoch. He called sin out for its face value. His preaching was not like the twenty first century charismatic preacher. These days among our preachers, it seems as if it's more about entertainment and emotions, rather than spiritual enrichment in our churches.

Today, we call sin "failure," or we say we've made "a mistake". We call pride "self-esteem", selfishness "fulfillment," lust "an instinct." If we cheat on our taxes, we call it "protecting our own interests." If we commit adultery, we call it "an endeavor to save the marriage." We call murdering an unborn child "terminating a pregnancy." But Enoch called sin, sin and evil, evil.

b) Enoch's Praise:

I can imagine Enoch's important agenda along with the burden of preaching was to praise God. There are seven types of praise in our Holy Bible, and with my sanctified imagination. I think Enoch imperatively fulfilled each of them. Let's look at each of them closely:

Yadah Praise - This means to worship with the extended hands, and to lift your hands unto the Lord. It carries the meaning of absolute surrender as a young child does to a parent, **"pick me up Lord, I'm all yours."**

Tehillah Praise - This means to sing out loud as if there's a violin in your voice. But! Perhaps if you can't say a word, "Just wave your hands."

Barak Praise - This means to kneel or to bow. Furthermore, this means to give reverence to God as an act of adoration.

Halal Praise - This means to make a show, or to boast in the Lord. The truth to the matter, "folks already have you on their gossiping list," so provide them with something more to talk about.

Towdah Praise - This mean to thank God before it's already done. The attitude for Towdah is, "I'm thanking God. I'm agreeing with God that it is as He says. I don't care what it looks like. I'm agreeing with what His Word says."

Zamar Praise - This means to sing with instruments. When you play the instrument; play them like it's your last time.

Shabach Praise - This means to address in a loud tone, a loud adoration, or a shout. Proclaim with a loud voice unashamed to exhibit the Lord.

If you want the same relationship that Enoch had with the Lord, you must learn how to Praise Him.

III. Enoch's Removal by God:

What happened to Enoch? "God took him." Nature did not take him. Disease did not take him. Death did not take him. The scripture says, "God took him." Enoch never tasted death as we know it. Enoch was born, he lived, and he ascended to heaven. Enoch's faith claimed the righteousness of God, and his faith looked upon the celestial city.

We are also preparing for God to come and take us for a walk, and in this preparation time. We need to be walking with Him as Enoch walked.

Chapter 11

⌒෴⌒

The Atoning Blood of Jesus

(Hebrew 9:22-26 KJV)

And almost all things are by the law purged with blood; and without shedding of blood is no remission. It was therefore necessary that the patterns of things in the heavens should be purified with these; but the heavenly things themselves with better sacrifices than these. For Christ is not entered into the holy places made with hands, which are the figures of the true; but into heaven itself, now to appear in the presence of God for us: Nor yet that he should offer himself often, as the high priest entereth into the holy place every year with blood of others; For then must he often have suffered since the foundation of the world: but now once in the end of the world hath he appeared to put away sin by the sacrifice of himself.

The Word of God has a scarlet red thread running through it. Like the cord Rahab hung out of her window. That scarlet thread, by which these sixty six books are bound together, which unifies everything written upon the pages of inspiration, is the precious living blood of Jesus Christ our redeemer.

The scriptures speak constantly about the blood. It is written in the books of the law, "*The life of the flesh is in the blood.*" God told Moses, "*The blood shall be to you for a token.*" He said, "*When I see the blood, I will pass over you*" (Exodus 12:13).

When the high priest went into the Holy of Holies on the Day of Atonement, he went in with the blood. The priest after entering into the Holy of Holies would sprinkle the blood on the Mercy Seat which rested upon the Ark of the Covenant.

When our Lord Jesus instituted the Lord's Supper, he took the cup of wine, held it before his disciples and said, *"This is the blood of the New Testament, shed for many for the remission of sins."* In (Hebrews 9:22), we read, *"Without shedding of blood is no remission of sin."* That makes the blood a matter of immense infinite importance.

Furthermore, Jesus is known by many titles but the most precious title of Christ is redeemer. It helps us to understand what it cost Him to get this salvation for us. It is the name specifically of the Christ of the cross. He is Christ our redeemer.

Whenever we say "redeemer," the cross is flashed before our eyes and our hearts are filled with loving remembrance not only that Christ has given us salvation, but the mighty price He paid for it.

When we deal with the subject matter of sin; we must understand that sin is serious according to Paul's writing to the Hebrews. Let us look closely at **The Seriousness of Sin** and then **The Sacrifice of a Savior**.

I. The Seriousness of Sin:

And almost all things are by the law purged with blood; and without shedding of blood is no remission (Hebrews 9:22).

According to the Bible we are slaves to sin and we cannot escape from this slavery. Sin is serious. "The wages of sin is death," sin alienates people from God, and all are sinners.

Sin is like acid, it will eat straight through who's carrying it. Sin is like a roach, it never comes out until company comes over. Sin is like a spider's web that clings to its prey once it trespasses its territory. Sin is like a blue runner snake, he'll chase you until he catches you.

However, Jesus has freed us from this sinful virus by going to the cross and paying our redemption by offering His precious blood. This is what the apostle Peter had in mind, (1 Peter 1:18-19), *"knowing that you were not redeemed with perishable things like silver or gold from your futile way of life inherited from your forefathers, but with precious blood, as of a lamb unblemished and spotless, the blood of Christ."*

II. The Sacrifice of a Savior:

(Hebrew 9:26)

For then must he often have suffered since the foundation of the world: but now once in the end of the world hath he appeared to put away sin by the sacrifice of himself.

The blood in Jesus body was not the magic. He had to die on a certain day and time, to fulfill the scriptures as the Passover Lamb. The blood of Christ refers to his sacrificial death. Literally, one can bleed and still not die but the Bible tells us he died for our sins by crucifixion.

In the Bible, blood signifies essentially the death, and is a clear expression of the death of Christ for our salvation. The blood is never mentioned except in connection, with the shedding of it, or with the use of it after it has been shed. The bloodshed is the life poured out, and the poured out life may be used only for atonement. Christ Jesus is our atoning sacrifice for sin.

It is impossible to escape the idea of the death of Christ being the high cost of our redemption. Christ's saving work involves His purchasing us for Himself in the world's marketplace, so that we never have to return there again.

John the baptizer introduced him as, "the Lamb that takes away the sins of the world." Christ fulfilled all the Old Testament types including the scapegoat but it was the Passover Lamb that was of the utmost importance. He was judged instead of us, so he passed over our judgment and we go from death to life.

The Passover Lamb of the Old Testament was only a picture of the ultimate sacrifice. When Jesus Christ went to the cross almost 2,000 years ago, He was the ultimate sacrifice.

- His skin was whipped off by scourging.
- His beard was torn out of his cheeks.
- His head pierced with thorns.
- His face was brutalized and marred.
- His hands and feet were nailed through with spikes.
- His side pierced with a spear after he died.

My God what a Blood Bath!

The sacrifice of Jesus Christ, the Son of God, completely abolished the system of animal sacrifice forever. The animal sacrifices of the Old Testament were only a picture, a figure, of the true sacrifice of Jesus Christ. Their blood was only a figure of the blood of Jesus that would be shed thousands of years later on a cross outside the city of Jerusalem.

Thank Jesus Christ for his precious atoning blood which speaks volumes of his Love emphatically.

There is a fountain filled with blood
Drawn from Immanuel's veins;
And sinners, plunged beneath that flood,
Lose all their guilty stains:

The dying thief rejoiced to see
That fountain in his day;

And there may I, though vile as he,
Wash all my sins away:

What can wash away my sin?
Nothing but the blood of Jesus;
What can make me whole again?
Nothing but the blood of Jesus.

When we are covered by the blood of Jesus, God sees us as completely pure and cleansed. We are made perfect in His site. Our relationship with Him is completely restored and we can come into His presence without any fear or doubt. If you are covered in the blood of Jesus, condemnation has no place in you.

Chapter 12

She's Cheating On Me

(Hosea 1:2 KJV)

The beginning of the word of the LORD by Hosea. And the LORD said to Hosea, Go, take unto thee a wife of whoredoms and children of whoredoms: for the land hath committed great whoredom, departing from the LORD.

The wedding was amazing. I knew the marriage would not last. But I performed the ceremony anyway. After all, they were both children of the covenant and neither, God nor man forbade me from doing the wedding. So, what else could I do but make the best of it? Everyone constantly smiled, we sang a lot, and honestly it was a beautiful ceremony.

There were tears in many eyes; when I pronounced them husband and wife. One could almost forget the absence of understanding, trust, and commitment that should be present at every marriage.

The groom was different from the bride. He was so deep and thoughtful and she was so shallow, superficial and surface. He was principled and she was dishonorable. As amazing as it sounds, he loved her. He loved her more than any other groom has ever loved a bride.

In his love he pursued her, and tried to help her. But she despised him for that help. More than once she threatened to leave him. She called his detection bothersome, invasive, painful, and unnecessary. She not only despised his extraordinary love, she publicly ridiculed it and defended her own superficial love as being real love. Yet, he pursued her anyway.

Many claimed to have seen her with another man; actually with a number of other men. She laughed at anyone who questioned her about this allegation.

I wondered what he saw in her. I didn't see anything in her to warrant such love, and such pursuit. No one who knew them both could think of a single reason he should want her. In fact, if anyone was marriage material, it was him and not her. He was the kind of guy every woman dreams of being the wind beneath his wings.

That's why the wedding was so amazing. Despite her commitment to shallowness, he pursued after her. He knew what she was doing and what she was like, and yet he still allowed her to manipulate his vulnerability.

This bride and groom, I am talking about is Hosea, the son of Beeri, and the unfastened woman Gomer, the daughter of Diblaim.

There are commentators who say their marriage never actually took place. The story, they say, is an allegory or parable, like the story Nathan told David about the rich man who took the poor man's only lamb. Many say the story is a vision or dream, like the dream Peter had of the unclean animals on a great sheet. In contrast, the Bible leads us to believe that the prophet really did enter into an unhappy marriage with an insignificant woman.

Why this marriage? The Word of God as preached was no longer making any impression upon Israel. And no one listened to the prophets of God anymore. Therefore the spoken word had to be reinforced or punctuated by deeds, and by a word acted out.

The Israelites are the bride of Christ, and this bride paid little or no attention when Hosea said, "This is what the Lord says." After all, words were cheap and there were other prophets, many of them false, claiming to speak the word of the Lord. But a marriage between a prophet of the Lord and a meaningless woman, especially one who later ran away from her husband, made everyone sit up and pay attention. Everyone buzzed with gossip; we can well imagine that the marriage quickly became one of the favorite topics of conversation.

This was exactly God's purpose. Once everyone was talking about the scandal, and had a chance to express a holier-than-thou attitude about the meaningless woman Hosea had chosen as his wife, Hosea could speak up and say, "You people are just like that unfaithful wife of mine, In the eyes of the Lord God Almighty."

I. The Agony of Hosea:

The marriage of Hosea and Gomer was a forced marriage, what in former times was called a "shotgun wedding." It was not forced in the sense that the bride was pregnant. It was forced in the sense that God ordered Hosea to marry Gomer. Hosea was given no choice in the matter.

God decreed that Hosea must marry a woman whose character was the complete opposite of his own. This is the big tragedy of Hosea's life. Gomer was simply unwilling or unable to be faithful and loving. She turned her love life into a soap opera. She threw herself into the arms of other men causing her husband great pain. She certainly earned her reputation as an adulterous woman!

"Go," says God, "take to your-self an adulterous wife." This tells us that Gomer was known as a woman of questionable morals even before Hosea asked for her hand in marriage. She was known for sleeping around, and for being fast and easy.

If you are familiar with this story, it appears that for a while everything appeared to be going well in the new home. Hosea and Gomer were blessed with the birth of a son. But the happiness, if any, did not last long. Gomer gave birth to two more children but these were children of adultery. Hosea knew that he was not the father, though he did love and accept them as if they were his own.

How painful it must have been for Hosea to discover that Gomer was unfaithful. People in that situation, all tell me how devastating it is when someone breaks your trust, betrays your love, and tramples on your passion.

To make matters worse, Gomer ran away. Hosea went after his adulterous wife to bring her back home. Why? You may ask, because the Lord commanded him not only to marry Gomer, but also to love her.

If only Hosea were free of that woman. If only he could let her go. That's just what he couldn't do; what he was not allowed to do. He had to marry her. He had to remain faithful to her. He had to love her and he did with all the self surrendering love of his tender heart.

We are being given a message here, of God's desire for marriage. God's will is that marriage be permanent. God's will is that marriages even survive adultery. This is the way God has intended marriages since the beginning. The current attitude, both inside and outside of the church, is that the marriage relationship is automatically broken if either partner is unfaithful or unloving. But Hosea shows us this doesn't have to be the case. Hosea reminds us this certainly is not the Lord's will.

No matter what Gomer did, regardless of the number of lovers she took on, Hosea loved her and was faithful to her. Hosea stuck with his wife despite the pain and agony she caused him.

II. The Agony of God:

The unhappy marriage of Hosea and Gomer is an illustration, a vivid picture of the relationship between God and His people. The Lord chose Israel as His bride. He loved her just like a groom loves His bride. He demonstrated that love in all sorts of ways such as freedom, victory, land, peace, prosperity, temple, worship, grace, and salvation. The Lord pampered and spoiled His bride with His openhandedness.

What did Israel do? How did she respond to God's love? Listen to the Lord's complaint, "the land is guilty of the vilest adultery in departing from the Lord."

Israel did exactly what Gomer did, even though she was quick to gossip, and judge, and condemn Gomer's unfaithfulness. But isn't that how it usually goes? All of us have a sharp eye for the sins of others, but we don't seem to notice our own.

Israel was completely blind to her own sin. Yet sin, she did. She chased after Baal and sought assistance from foreign kings instead of the Lord, using the language of Hosea we would have to call this spiritual adultery. Yet, at the same time she continued her worship of the Lord. Imagine chasing after the Baal and worshiping the Lord at the same time. Israel didn't just commit adultery! We would have to accuse her of bigamy; trying to have two husbands at the same time.

The Lord is a jealous God, a jealous husband, and He despised the worship of Israel. It is Him or nothing. It is Him and no other. Israel tried to put God in the same classification as her other lovers.

I spoke earlier of Hosea and the pain the marriage to Gomer caused him. Instead of looking to Hosea and his pain we are to look at God's pain. You see, Hosea's pain is but a portrait of God's pain. By forcing Hosea to marry and stay married to Gomer, the Lord was making Hosea feel some of the pain. He himself suffered because of his unfaithful people. Our passage, when it comes right down to it is about God's wounded love.

The real pain in our passage is God. God had to watch His people, the bride He had chosen for Himself, become unfaithful and desert Him to chase after Baal. Just like adultery hurts us and Hosea, so it also hurts the Lord.

We can say the same thing about the church that we said about Israel. The Lord has chosen the church as His bride. He loves her just like a groom loves His bride. He demonstrates His love in all sorts of ways, such as freedom, victory, peace, worship, grace, salvation, forgiveness, redemption, and eternal life.

How do we respond to God's love? Are we any better than the Israelites of Hosea's time? Like Israel, it is easy to condemn those who openly live in sin; but do we realize that our relationship with God is just as flawed?

Who for instance, would ever dare to claim that we have always and at all times put the Lord first in our lives?

In a good marriage, the husband and wife are supposed to live with each other and not just sleep beside each other. There is supposed to be a living, loving relationship in every sense of the term, but there are thousands who don't live that way with God. They live beside Him instead of with Him. Their relationship with the Lord is not a permanent exclusive partnership of love and fidelity. They are busy looking in all directions, instead of looking to God.

Look to God, and spend time with Him. Spending time with God doesn't need to be difficult. In many ways, spending time with God is a bit like exercising. Many people find that when they begin an exercise program, the "fun" stage quickly wears off and it requires a lot of discipline to keep at it. But for those who do stick with it through this tough time, exercising regularly becomes fun, comes easy, and they can't imagine wanting to go without it.

Chapter 13

✧

Can These Bones Live?

(Ezekiel 37:1-14 KJV)

*And he said unto me, Son of man, can these bones live? And
I answered, O Lord GOD, thou knowest.*

Ezekiel was a priest and prophet who lived in the sixth century B.C.
during the Babylonian exile. The Jews had been conquered by the
Babylonian army, taken captive and brought hundreds of miles to
Babylon. This is where the prophet Ezekiel held his preaching ministry to
the Jewish community in exile.

In our passage today, he had a vision where the hand of the Lord took
him up and sat him down in a large open valley filled with dry bones.

This was an ancient battlefield, and these were the bones of soldiers.
These were the remains of Jewish warriors who had died fighting the
Babylonians on one of the largest battlefields of Israel, perhaps even the
famous valley of Megiddo, known as Armageddon.

The Jews had been defeated so badly that there was no one left to bury
their fallen soldiers, so their bodies lay in the fields until all that was left
were bones.

The Lord took Ezekiel in the spirit and sat him down in that battlefield,
the place of Jewish defeat and death. He gave him a tour of the place.

"Then He caused me to pass by them all around, and behold, there were very many in the open valley; and indeed they were very dry." God asked Ezekiel the question, ""Son of man, can these bones live?" And Ezekiel answered, "Who knows? O Lord only You know" (Ezekiel 37:2-3).

Israel was defeated, captive, deported, and enslaved with no prospect of returning to the land. The Jews did not have any certainty that their nation would ever rise again. The people were losing hope is what Ezekiel was voicing here.

Ezekiel speaks for all people who are discouraged, depressed, and beaten down. A lot of things can beat us down so that we feel like there is no possibility of us ever getting back up on our feet again. Life can beat us up and defeat us, just like these soldiers in this valley were defeated. Life can deal us very severe blows.

We evaluate our finances, our jobs, our marriages, our families, our health, our hearts, minds and souls. Financially, emotionally, and spiritually we can feel like we have no more life in us than the dry bones in this valley; No more of a chance at having life again than these bones had of coming back to life.

The question to Ezekiel was, "Can these bones live?" The answer is "Yes!" Though it seems impossible, with God all things are possible. How can life come to dry bones? There are seven answers to this question.

I. First, Life comes by the Word of God:

Again He said to me, Prophesy to these bones, and say to them, O dry bones, hear the word of the LORD! Thus says the Lord GOD to these bones: "Surely I will cause breath to enter into you, and you shall live." I will put sinews (a tough band of fibrous connective tissue that usually connects muscle to bone) on you and bring flesh upon you, cover you with skin and put breath in you; and you shall live. Then you shall know that I am the LORD (Ezekiel 37:4-8).

So, I prophesied as I was commanded and as I prophesied, there was a noise, and suddenly a rattling and the bones came together bone to bone. As I looked, the sinews and the flesh came upon them, and the skin covered them over.

Visualize this tremendous sight with me. God tells the prophet to prophesy to the bones. He tells this prophet to preach to people who are dead; not like Jesus speaking to Lazarus who had only been dead in the tomb four days.

These people had been dead for decades. Their bones were dry. As verse 2 says "*indeed they were very dry.*" Ezekiel had a large congregation that day. It says the valley "was full of bones, there were very many in the open valley." There wasn't enough room in the attendance books to record the names of all the people present to hear Ezekiel preach in that day, but, they were dead!

This valley was undoubtedly beautiful outdoor scenery. Ezekiel had thousands of people in attendance. Ezekiel stood outside with a crowd of people before him. God told him to preach to this congregation. You are talking about a dead church! This is exactly what Ezekiel experienced but we must realize that this is a vision that communicates a spiritual truth.

II. Life comes by the Proclamation of the Word:

"How then shall they call on him in whom they have not believed? and how shall they believe in him of whom they have not heard? and how shall they hear without a preacher? And how shall they preach, except they be sent? as it is written, How beautiful are the feet of them that preach the gospel of peace, and bring glad tidings of good things! But they have not all obeyed the gospel. For Esaias saith, Lord, who hath believed our report? So then faith cometh by hearing, and hearing by the word of God" (Romans 10:14-17).

There is no life without the proclamation of the Word of life. The Word of God doesn't come to live people who respond to become better people. The Word of God comes to dead people to make them alive. Life comes by the Proclamation of the Word.

III. Life comes by hearing of the Word:

God told Ezekiel that his message to the bones was that they should listen. "O dry bones, hear the word of the Lord!" How can dry bones hear the word of the Lord? They are just bones. They have no ears! There is no flesh on them! How can you hear without ears?

It gives a whole new meaning to the words that Jesus repeated often:

"He, who has ears to hear, let him hear." These bones literally had no ears to hear. So God gave them ears. Then we have this dramatic scene when Ezekiel preached as he was commanded and as he was preaching he heard a rattling in the congregation.

While Ezekiel was preaching he heard a noise in his congregation similar to a rattling noise. Verse seven *"So I prophesied as I was commanded; and as I prophesied, there was a noise, and suddenly a rattling."* The rattling noise was the sound of the dead dry bones moving and coming together. You know the lyrics to the old song!

- The head bone connected to the neck bone.
- The neck bone connected to the shoulder bone.
- The shoulder bone connected to the back bone.
- The back bone connected to the hip bone.
- The hip bone connected to the thigh bone.
- The thigh bone connected to the knee bone.
- The knee bone connected to the shin bone.
- The shin bone connected to the ankle bone.
- The ankle bone finally connected to the foot bone.

Now hear the Word of the Lord!

The bones were connecting to each other. Soon, Ezekiel had a bunch of skeletons before him. Then, God put flesh and skin on them, so he had a bunch of dead bodies sitting in his congregation. But it says in verse eight *"Indeed, as I looked, the sinews and the flesh came upon them, and the skin covered them over; but there was no breath in them."* They were flesh and blood but no life. They had ears now, but they could not hear. Life comes by proclamation of the Word. Life comes by hearing the Word. But, still there was no life yet. One thing was missing.

IV. Life comes by the Spirit of God:

"Also He said to me, "Prophesy to the breath, prophesy, son of man, and say to the breath, 'Thus says the Lord GOD: "Come from the four winds, O breath, and breathe on these slain, that they may live. So I prophesied as He commanded me, and breath came into them, and they lived, and stood upon their feet, an exceedingly great army" (Ezekiel 37: 9).

In Hebrew; which is the language the Old Testament was written in, the word for breath is exactly the same word as wind or spirit. This can be translated in any of these three ways. In fact there are different published translations that say "Prophesy to the breath" or "Prophesy to the wind" or "Prophesy to the spirit."

Ezekiel had in mind the creation story of Genesis chapter two. There it says that God made man's body out of the dust of the earth and then that he "breathed into his nostrils the breath of life and he became a living soul." That's how God created man in the beginning.

God was recreating man in the text. Ezekiel preached the Word of God and there was a sound of a mighty rushing wind, like Job and Elijah experienced. That wind was the breath of God, the spirit of the living God, which entered into those dead corpses.

Then all of a sudden all the bodies took one collective deep breath, and they all came alive. It says, "breath came into them, and they lived, and stood upon their feet, an exceedingly great army." Life comes by the Spirit of the Lord and Spiritual life comes only by the power of the Holy Spirit. What is the meaning of this new life given to these dry bones?

V. This life means Hope:

Then he said unto me, Son of man, these bones are the whole house of Israel: behold, they say, Our bones are dried, and our hope is lost: we are cut off for our parts (Ezekiel 37: 11).

These bones represented the people and the nation of Israel. The people of Israel were without hope. They were a conquered defeated people, refugees in a foreign land. Their homeland had been destroyed, the capital of Jerusalem leveled, and the temple demolished. They had no hope that they would ever have anything like the life they once possessed.

They felt like their life was over and they felt hopeless, but, God by his Word and by his Spirit can bring hope. This is true for us as well. Maybe you feel hopeless for any number of reasons. The Word of God and the Spirit of God can bring you hope.

VI. This life means Return:

Therefore prophesy and say unto them, Thus saith the Lord GOD; Behold, O my people, I will open your graves, and cause you to come up out of your graves, and bring you into the land of Israel. And shall put my spirit in you, and ye shall live, and I shall place you in your own land: then shall ye know that I the LORD have spoken it, and performed it, saith the LORD (Ezekiel 37: 12, 14).

This vision meant that God was going to bring the Jews back to their land. And he did. It was a promise of a return.

VII. This life means Resurrection:

This story of the valley of dry bones is a prophecy of the resurrection day.

And ye shall know that I am the LORD, when I have opened your graves, O my people, and brought you up out of your graves, (Ezekiel 37: 13).

There is more in this prophecy than a return to the land of Israel for the Jews in exile. There is a promise of resurrection from the grave. Though we die, we shall live because there is life beyond death as Jesus said, *"He who believes in me though he die, yet shall he live."* Unless we are among those on earth when the last trumpet sounds and the Lord descends and transforms our mortal bodies in a twinkling of an eye, unless we are of that last generation, we will die as generations of Christians have died before us. Our bodies will turn to dust, our bones as dry as these bones in the valley of dry bones. Yet shall we will live again!

It is too easy to live in hopelessness when we see and feel dry bones all around us. But in the presence of God anything is possible - stay out of His way and watch as dry bones rise up again in the presence of and by the power of God

Chapter 14

⟶⟶

The Pastor's Love Day

(Matthew 26:6-13 KJV)

Now when Jesus was in Bethany, in the house of Simon the leper, There came unto him a woman having an alabaster box of very precious ointment, and poured it on his head, as he sat at meat. But when his disciples saw it, they had indignation, saying, To what purpose is this waste? For this ointment might have been sold for much, and given to the poor. When Jesus understood it, he said unto them, Why trouble ye the woman? for she hath wrought a good work upon me. For ye have the poor always with you; but me ye have not always. For in that she hath poured this ointment on my body, she did it for my burial. Verily I say unto you, Wheresoever this gospel shall be preached in the whole world, there shall also this, that this woman hath done, be told for a memorial of her.

One day Jesus was in Bethany at the home of a man known as Simon the Leper. Jesus was probably there because the family wanted to thank Him for curing Simon's leprosy. While entertaining each other something unusual happens, that surprises everyone. A woman with strange unethical uncustomary conduct appears out of nowhere and startles the guests.

I. The Conduct of this Woman:

Now when Jesus was in Bethany, in the house of Simon the leper, There came unto him a woman having an alabaster box of very precious ointment, and poured it on his head, as he sat at meat (Matthew 26:6-7).

While Jesus was reclining at the table, enjoying the food and company of His friends, and disciples, this woman entered in and couldn't restrain herself from Jesus. She had to express her love and devotion to Him. So, she took a flask of perfume and broke the neck of the expensive marble jar and poured the perfume on Him.

This lowly woman was just like what the 21st century church folks call; a second-class citizen in a forgotten Roman occupied territory. There was no earthly reason for anyone to commend her, let alone listen to her. And yet this woman stood in the gap and organized a last minute love day for Jesus who well deserved to be the honoree. However, she couldn't honor a man like Jesus who already owned everything, but it was the thought that counted the most.

It wasn't Samuel who came with his oil to anoint this King of kings. It wasn't the chief priests who were so heavenly minded, that they were no earthly good, nor was it the wisest of the Pharisees who came to anoint the Messiah.

Instead, a humble woman came in with her love for Jesus and broke over his head what was probably her most precious earthly possession.

II. The Cost of this Gift:

But when his disciples saw it, they had indignation, saying, To what purpose is this waste? For this ointment might have been sold for much, and given to the poor (Matthew 26:8-9).

a) **It Cost Her Currency:**

The Gospel of Mark, he tells us it represented more than a year's wages.

For it might have been sold for more than three hundred pence, and have been given to the poor. And they murmured against her (Mark 14:5).

The disciples became angry. Surprised by the selfless act, their first concern was over the purchase price of what was sacrificed, rather than the act itself. This woman had freely poured out her treasure on Jesus. From a heart of faith she anointed his head with oil.

b) **It Cost Her Criticism:**

The disciples judged her with a critical eye; while using the poor as an excuse they hid what really offended them. What they were really angry about was the excess of her sacrifice and that she had emptied all of it on Jesus.

I can hear Judas getting all this drama kicked off and disturbing the other brethrens by saying, "Jesus isn't worth breaking the whole flask over Him?" She should have given Him a few drops, "It would have been better to sell the perfume to support the poor." "It really doesn't take all that for Jesus. He puts his pants on just like we do." What disrespect, what a bad comment to interject concerning the leader among the others who followed Jesus' leadership.

How often are Christians mocked for doing too much rather than too little? What was done to Jesus by this woman will stand as an eternal example for us. We too should pour out our hearts in love as well. We too should be inspired to exercise our faith giving generously, even if it's embarrassing.

Here is Judas, who wanted to be in charge. He was not interested in listening to neither Jesus nor any disciple who were strong supporters of

Jesus. Judas wanted to dictate how things are to be handled, as well as when they should be accomplished. Judas wanted his opinions valued and he wanted his values respected. Judas wanted his concerns taken seriously. If nothing else, Judas wanted to call the shots to be sure no one else is calling them.

I wonder if there are any Judas' still lurking within our churches? I pray they experience Jesus; the next time the doors are open for authentic worship.

Joshua suggested to the children of Israel *"As for me and my house we will serve the Lord* (Joshua 24:15)" Stop listening to Judas' in the church and serve the Lord.

He wasn't a team player, but a team persecutor of Leadership. If things weren't his way; he held hostage a serious attitude. Judas was an instigator who planted and grew, the seed of discourse in the hearts of the others, and all of this was over money. Instead of giving Jesus something out of the ministry bag for Jesus' love day celebration. He complained about what the woman gave. What was he really saying? He was saying, "Jesus wasn't worth a dime!" He didn't value Jesus' leadership.

In this day and time people do not value and know what it is to be an effective Pastor. It is a dangerous job. Pastoring isn't easy! Here's a short list of his responsibilities.

The Pastoral Duties:

He must pray and study the scriptures, oversee and lead the church, act by Gods authority, teach the bible correctly, preach the uncompromising gospel, visit and pray for the sick, and rightly use money and power. He must protect the church from false teachers, discipline unrepentant Christians, developing other leaders and teachers, watch over every member of the flock, and visit the flock to know their state. A Pastor must administer the ordinances of the church, perform marriages and home-going services, model Christ likeness, love the people although some don't care for him, pray down heaven's glory, quench hell's fire, promote family religion and prepare and deliver sermons. He must also assist in church financial matters, oversee management of all areas of the congregation's ministry, support, oversee and evaluate congregational staff, hold regular staff meetings to coordinate ministries, and try to stay alive while doing all that!

III. The Compliment of this Gift:

When Jesus understood it, he said unto them, Why trouble ye the woman? for she hath wrought a good work upon me. For ye have the poor always with you; but me ye have not always. For in that she hath poured this ointment on my body, she did it for my burial. Verily I say unto you, Wheresoever this gospel shall be preached in the whole world, there shall also this, that this woman hath done, be told for a memorial of her (Matthew: 26:10-13).

The Lord of the Universe is now dripping with perfume. He commends her, and the woman is praised in the presence of Jesus and his disciples. Although, the matter simply could have ended there, Jesus went on.

He wanted to teach us something about the deeper beauties of this woman. She had anointed him for the death-shattering task he would face in just three days. In her gift of love, this woman prepared the Son of the Living God, for the tomb. A tomb that would try to hold him, but wouldn't. It would be a tomb that would try to claim him, but couldn't keep Him.

Remember, nothing makes the journey more enjoyable than ministering to members that love their pastor as he loves them. I heard a story concerning a pastor that was struggling with discouragement. He had left a successful business to oversee a fledgling flock. In 10 years, his leadership helped them get out of crippling debt, quadruple the church attendance, move into an attractive building, and internally strengthen discipleship and membership. He did not receive a raise, and at his 10 year celebration, the church gave him a plaque and a cake. Thankfully, he will one day receive his due appreciation. (1 Peter 5:4) says, *"And when the chief Shepherd shall appear, ye shall receive a crown of glory that fadeth not away."*

Chapter 15

⌒ルⱺ

He Did It for Us

(John 3:16; 1 John 3:16 KJV)

"For God so loved the world that He gave His only begotten Son, that whoever believes in Him should not perish but have everlasting life" (John 3:16).

"By this we have known the love of God, because He laid down His life for us. And we ought to lay down our lives for the brothers" (1 John 3:16).

The first similarity is that both verses are talking about the same event; the death of Jesus on the Cross. Secondly, they both talk about the love necessary to carry out this event, but notice one very important difference between the two:

- John 3:16 is told from the perspective of the Father.
- 1 John 3:16 focuses instead of what the Son went through.

I can't imagine how difficult it would be to allow my son to die such a brutal death; even if I were assured beforehand that he would be alive again in just three days. Yet, John 3:16 tells us that God the Father of Jesus was willing to make this sacrifice and the reason why; love was His motivation, *"For God so loved the world that He gave His only begotten Son, that whoever believes in Him should not perish but have everlasting life"* (John 3:16).

At the same time, I cannot imagine what kind of love Jesus must have had to be willing to die for people, He didn't know. Again, this verse tells us He was motivated by love.

When God gave Jesus to us, He gave His all! He gave Himself.

> *"For God so loved the world that He gave his only Son, that whoever believes in him should not perish but have eternal life"* (John 3:16).

This argument has a few points:

- **The Giver:** First of all, consider who the Giver is. The same God who created the whole world in the beginning continues to give the whole world what it needs.
- **The Motive:** Secondly, consider the motive that moves God to do what He does. *"For God so loved"* His motive is love, pure, perfect love. The bible calls love the highest and greatest of all virtues. Love is not temporary or on again, off again, "love never ends."

Imagine your son or daughter who has committed a crime against society but has yet to be proven guilty. Love will make you get on the phone and solicit help to get him or her out solitary confinement.

Love makes you see no wrong in him. Although you knew they were guilty of the crime. Love will make you defend them when others are trying to destroy them. There's a thin line between love and hate! Love will make a jealous individual, put tires on flat, sugar in gas tanks, and set clothes on fire. But wait one minute, when we sinned against God, He allowed Jesus to do what no other man could do.

"But God commendeth his love toward us, in that, while we were yet sinners, Christ died for us" (Romans 5:8).

- **The Magnitude:** Thirdly, considers the magnitude of the gift. *"For God so loved the world, that He gave His only Son."* What greater gift could God give than His own Son? The Son is everything to the Father and He is the expressed image of His Father. By the gift of His Son, God gives us Himself.

Think about God's loving gift of kindness to you through your entire life.

- He has carried you all your life.
- He has been with you in your difficult times.
- He has kept you safe during the storms and trials of your life.
- He has been so good and merciful to you in spite of your unfaithfulness.

- **He Gave:** Fourthly, consider that little word "gave" "God gave His only Son." What an important word!

"For unto us a child is born, unto us a son is given: and the government shall be upon his shoulder: and his name shall be called Wonderful, Counsellor, The mighty God, The everlasting Father, The Prince of Peace" (Isaiah 9:6).

Wages are paid, possessions are purchased, homes are mortgaged and cars are financed, but gifts are given. He gave His only Son because this is what love does. Love gives!

- **The Recipient:** Fifthly, consider to whom God gives this most Holy and precious gift of His only Son. *"God so loved the world that He gave His only Son."* We have a very hard time with that one. There's got to be something not quite right about that.

Parenthetically, "we love what we consider lovely or loveable." When we're single, we look for someone whom we love or can love and we try to marry them. When we are house shopping or clothes shopping we look for something we like. It's got to be what we're looking for or at least close. When we find it we buy it or mortgage it or charge it. With us, we find a worthy object of our love and to love.

- **The Purpose:** Sixth and last point, consider the purpose of this gift. He gives His Son, *"so that whoever believes in Him should not perish but have eternal life."* His purpose is not to harm you or to condemn the world. The world does a fine enough job of that all by itself. Nor is it His purpose to make you healthy, wealthy and wise, or to give you success, honor and power. You can have all of these things and still be under the rule of the devil and take them all to hell with you. God's pure love has given the gift of His Son to crush the serpent's head, open the gates of heaven and prepare a place for you in His Father's house to live forever.

God's purpose in putting the serpent on the pole was that those who were dying might look at it and live. God's purpose never changes. Now, He has lifted up His Son on the cross so that by grace alone and through faith alone, you would believe in Him and have eternal life.

Now, take a good, long look at the Man on the Cross, Jesus Christ. He is bleeding; dark clouds are rolling down from heaven, clothing the world in darkness. Look up, at His face and see the anguish, pain, blood, tears, mouth gasping for breath.

He is covered in His own blood, plunged into the uttermost depths of grief. It was for us all this happened. Jesus Christ did all this for us. The night in the Garden spent in prayer, Pilate's court, the insults, being spit upon, a crown of thorns shoved on His head, scourged until flesh hung from His back, then a heavy cross to carry. He did it all for us!

While hanging from that cross hear Him give eternal life to the man on a cross next to Him. Hear Him call to His mother, and hear Him call out for something to drink. Who would do such a thing to another human being? Whoever did this deserves the same treatment as they had given this man, but it had to be done in order that our sins could be forgiven.

God says through his divinely inspired Scriptures that somehow Jesus' death was my death and your death. We were helpless, spiritually dead, and separated from God. Yet, when Jesus died on the cross, his death was somehow ours so that we don't have to be separated from God anymore. We no longer have to be lost in a maze of self-centeredness, living for ourselves. Because Jesus' death was our death, we can live like, with, and for Jesus, spiritually alive and connected to the living God.

Chapter 16

⁓

Stop Playing Church

(Exodus 33:1-3 KJV)

And the LORD said unto Moses, Depart, and go up hence, thou and the people which thou hast brought up out of the land of Egypt, unto the land which I sware unto Abraham, to Isaac, and to Jacob, saying, Unto thy seed will I give it: And I will send an angel before thee; and I will drive out the Canaanite, the Amorite, and the Hittite, and the Perizzite, the Hivite, and the Jebusite: Unto a land flowing with milk and honey: for I will not go up in the midst of thee; for thou art a stiffnecked people: lest I consume thee in the way.

Worship is enjoying the presence of God. We respond to God with worship, because worship is simply giving God what is fitting. He is praiseworthy, not only for his power but also for his compassion.

Worship is a way of life. We offer our bodies and minds as living sacrifices (Romans 12:1-2). We worship God when we share the gospel (Romans 15:16). We worship God when we give financial offerings (Philippians 4:18). We worship God when we help other people (Hebrews 13:16). We say that he is worthy, worth our time, attention, and allegiance. We praise his glory, and his humility in becoming one of us for our sakes. We praise his righteousness and his mercy. We praise him for the way He really is.

In (Exodus 33:1-3), God gave the children of Israel His protection, provision, and His promise, but not His presence. The reason God exempted His presence was because of their worship.

God had authorized Moses to move forward with the plans of leading the children of Israel toward the promise land. God specifically informed Moses; He would not provide His presence because of their immorality.

God is omnipresence, but what really aggravated God to the point that He preferred not to provide His Shekinah Glory amongst His chosen people?

I. The Despicable Crime:

And he received them at their hand, and fashioned it with a graving tool, after he had made it a molten calf: and they said, These be thy gods, O Israel, which brought thee up out of the land of Egypt. And when Aaron saw it, he built an altar before it; and Aaron made proclamation, and said, To morrow is a feast to the LORD. And they rose up early on the morrow, and offered burnt offerings, and brought peace offerings; and the people sat down to eat and to drink, and rose up to play. And the LORD said unto Moses, Go, get thee down; for thy people, which thou broughtest out of the land of Egypt, have corrupted themselves: They have turned aside quickly out of the way which I commanded them: they have made them a molten calf, and have worshipped it, and have sacrificed thereunto, and said, These be thy gods, O Israel, which have brought thee up out of the land of Egypt. And the LORD said unto Moses, I have seen this people, and, behold, it is a stiffnecked people: Now therefore let me alone, that my wrath may wax hot against them, and that I may consume them: and I will make of thee a great nation (Exodus 32:4-10).

Moses was upon Mt. Sinai to receive the Ten Commandments from the Lord. In the absent of Moses, his brother Aaron led the people in a revolt against God. The people gave Aaron their bracelets and earrings; out of which Aaron made a golden calf that the people worshiped. Due to their sin, the Lord decided to remove His presence from them. He would give the people His shelter and shield. He would fulfill His promise to give them the land of Canaan. But He would not go with them into the land.

These people were considered Gods children. He watched over them; even though he was an invisible God. He still illuminated his protection, provision and presence, despite their conditions, because of the intermediary Moses their leader.

II. The Dispensed Consequences:

And it came to pass on the morrow, that Moses said unto the people, Ye have sinned a great sin: and now I will go up unto the LORD; peradventure I shall make an atonement for your sin. And Moses returned unto the LORD, and said, Oh, this people have sinned a great sin, and have made them gods of gold. Yet now, if thou wilt forgive their sin--; and if not, blot me, I pray thee, out of thy book which thou hast written (Exodus 32:30-32).

Moses descends the mountain, and sees the idolatry and immorality among the Israelites. He breaks the Ten Commandments, melts down and grinds the Golden Calf into powder, mixes it with water and forces the people to drink of it! Moses rebukes Aaron and orders the Levites to kill three thousand of the primary troublemakers.

III. The Direct Command:

And the LORD said unto Moses, Depart, and go up hence, thou and the people which thou hast brought up out of the land of Egypt, unto the land which I sware unto Abraham, to Isaac, and to Jacob, saying, Unto thy seed will I give it: And I will send an angel before thee; and I will drive out the Canaanite, the Amorite, and the Hittite, and the Perizzite, the Hivite, and the Jebusite: Unto a land flowing with milk and honey: for I will not go up in the midst of thee; for thou art a stiffnecked people: lest I consume thee in the way. And when the people heard these evil tidings, they mourned: and no man did put on him his ornaments (Exodus 33:1-4).

Many Christians today do not have the conscious presence of God in their lives. They are going about establishing their own righteousness but not according to Gods righteousness.

As children of God we shouldn't settle only for God's protection, His provision, or even the Promised Land, without His presence. When you have the presence of God, you need nothing more, and you should settle for nothing less.

There are four things that will rob us of God manifested presence in our lives; which are the archenemy of worship.

- **Direct Disobedience:**

And the LORD said unto Moses, Go, get thee down; for thy people, which thou broughtest out of the land of Egypt, have corrupted themselves: They have turned aside quickly out of the way which I commanded them: they have made them a molten calf, and have worshipped it, and have sacrificed thereunto, and said, These be thy gods, O Israel, which have brought thee up out of the land of Egypt (Exodus 32:7-8).

Many people confess faith in the Lord Jesus, but do not have His presence in their lives. And they do not have the assurance of their salvation. When we willingly and knowingly disobey God, we grieve the Holy Spirit. When we grieve the Holy Spirit, we then quench the Spirit. The Holy Spirit is to us what the pillar of cloud and fire was to the children of Israel.

And the LORD went before them by day in a pillar of a cloud, to lead them the way; and by night in a pillar of fire, to give them light; to go by day and night: He took not away the pillar of the cloud by day, nor the pillar of fire by night, from before the people (Exodus 13:21-22).

The Holy Spirit is God's manifested presence in our lives. When we deliberately disobey God, we grieve the Spirit and quench the Spirit, and when we do that, God ceases to be real in our lives.

- **Divided Devotion: (Exodus 32:4)**

The Golden Calf caused a Divided Devotion. An idol is anything we love more, fear more, serve more, and trust more than God.

- Is there anyone or anything that takes precedence over God in your life?
- Is there anyone or anything that is a greater controlling factor of your behavior than God?
- Is there a relationship that means more to you?
- Is there a treasure that means more to you?
- Is there anything that gets more of your attention than God?

- **Displaced Dependence:**

They have turned aside quickly out of the way which I commanded them: they have made them a molten calf, and have worshipped it, and have sacrificed thereunto, and said, These be thy gods, O Israel, which have brought thee up out of the land of Egypt (Exodus 32: 8).

When God gives us a victory and we give the glory to someone or something else, we then depend upon that other person or thing rather than upon God, and we will lose the presence of God in our lives.

- **Determined Defiance:**

And the LORD said unto Moses, I have seen this people, and, behold, it is a stiffnecked people: (Exodus 32:9).

"**Stiff necked**" is the opposite of being meek and pliable.

- Is there someone God has laid on your heart to witness to, but you haven't witnessed to that person?
- Has God given you an impulse to serve in a specific capacity, but you have refused?
- Has God laid something on your heart that He wants you to give?
- Has God laid someone on your heart with whom you need to apologize to and to reconcile?
- Has God been telling you that there is a wrong relationship in your life that you need to break off?

Moses did not want to go without the Lord's presence:

And he said unto him, If thy presence go not with me, carry us not up hence (Exodus 33:15).

Do not settle for anything less than God's presence in your life.

- God needs **workers** who will pick up their tools and work at any cost!
- God needs **warriors** who are willing to fight at any cost!
- God needs **worshipers** who are willing to worship him at any cost!

The purpose of our worship is to glorify, honor, praise, exalt, and please God. Our worship must show our adoration and loyalty to God for His grace in providing us with the way to escape the bondage of sin, so we can have the salvation He so much wants to give us. The nature of the worship God demands is the prostration of our souls before Him in humble and contrite submission. (James 4:6, 10) tells us, "*But he giveth more grace. Wherefore he saith, God resisteth the proud, but giveth grace unto the humble. Humble yourselves in the sight of the Lord, and he shall lift you up.* "Our worship to God should be is a very humble and reverent action.

Chapter 17

⚜

More Than Enough

(Numbers 11:5-6; 31-35 KJV)

We remember the fish, which we did eat in Egypt freely; the cucumbers, and the melons, and the leeks, and the onions, and the garlick: But now our soul is dried away: there is nothing at all, beside this manna, before our eyes (Numbers 11:5-6) .

And there went forth a wind from the LORD, and brought quails from the sea, and let them fall by the camp, as it were a day's journey on this side, and as it were a day's journey on the other side, round about the camp, and as it were two cubits high upon the face of the earth. And the people stood up all that day, and all that night, and all the next day, and they gathered the quails: he that gathered least gathered ten homers: and they spread them all abroad for themselves round about the camp. And while the flesh was yet between their teeth, ere it was chewed, the wrath of the LORD was kindled against the people, and the LORD smote the people with a very great plague. And he called the name of that place Kibrothhattaavah: because there they buried the people that lusted. And the people journeyed from Kibrothhattaavah unto Hazeroth; and abode at Hazeroth (Numbers 11:31-35).

Manna is a Hebrew word. Its literal meaning is, "what is it" or "whatchmacallit." It was a miraculous gift from God. Manna is interesting stuff. It looked like little beads or seeds, and frost like. This manna came every morning except the Sabbath. Its taste was like honey, or fresh oil. It also could be made into many different dishes and the children of Israel lived on it for forty years.

It was a complete food with all its vitamins and minerals. This manna was God miracle food. Absolutely, this was God's nourishing provision to see Israel though the wilderness experience. Today Jesus Christ is our provision. He's God's nourishment our journey.

I am that bread of life. Your fathers did eat manna in the wilderness, and are dead. This is the bread which cometh down from heaven, that a man may eat thereof, and not die (John 6:48-50).

Israel had just overcome a mighty victory of the Red Sea. Satan took a bad beating, but he didn't give up. Instead he laid a devious trap into the hearts of some and he was able to plant the seeds of discontent.

God was providing their every need, and Israel still complained. In fact, we as a people of God need to be on guard lest we fall into the same trap.

I. Notice when the Trap was Laid:

After a great victory!

Satan reserves his most devious, sneaking, cunning attacks for when we are reveling in a spiritual victory. When you have a victory don't dare relax. Don't get complacent. Don't think you have conquered Satan. Don't quit doing the things that brought you the victory. Pray when in battle, and pray just as fervently in victory.

Be Alert and expect an entrapment! The nature of Satan is completely opposite that of God. God is always good with no admixture of evil. He always acts to achieve what is best for all His creatures. Satan is always evil.

He may do what appears to be good, but if so, it is done with evil motives to achieve his own evil ends, not really to be of benefit to God or man.

II. Notice the Character of the Trap:

Satan causes a battle within the hearts of men!

I'm concerned for many of God's people. You have fought the unsettled battles of life, depended on God for your provisions and you trusted God in your darkest hours. But now the battle is over, you are prosperous, and you buy whatever you want. Immaturely, you don't have to trust God anymore. You have abandoned God. You have become subjective to Satan's trap of prosperity.

The Israelites were in need of water. So, God gave them drink. They needed food. So, the Lord fed them manna from heaven. Now that they have what they need they become discontented. They wanted the things of Egypt.

The Israelites wanted fish, but failed to realize they were in the desert, going around in circles. The Israelites ignored God's menu which required their faithfulness, and insisted on Egypt's menu which requested their fleshly desire.

Instead of remembering the miracles that God had performed before them, and praying to Him for food they desired. They put the blame on Moses and Aaron, and grumbled.

Instead of being thankful that they had been delivered from the bondage they were in. They sought the flesh that they had been cooking in their pots and eating. In essence they were saying that they wanted to go back to Egypt, the symbolic land of sin.

We must also remember that they were heading for another sinful land, Canaan, where the Lord was going to drive out the sinful people before them. The Lord wanted His people to be different, yet they were seeking to be the same.

III. Notice what Satan Attacked:

Satan attacked their appetite for God's bread. Satan attacked their thankfulness for his bread.

God's bread for the Israelites was Manna. It was a perfect food, even better than fish, cukes, garlic, quails. Yet, they were discontent with God's menu!

The raining down of Manna was the type and shadow of Jesus being rejected by the Jews. John said, *"He came unto his own, and his own received him not"* (John 1:11).

Jesus is the perfect bread for you. He is all you need. Satan's target is to replace your taste for God's bread with the world's spices. He says, "Look how tangy the worldly life is, and look how savory the materialistic life is" He plants a false vision of the good life in your mind, and you become dissatisfied with God's bread.

IV. Notice the Result of their Complaining about God's Provision:

The rabbles among the people still were not thankful for what the Lord had given them, and unless a stand is made against the rabble in a community. They have a tendency to discourage many of the other people to the point that they too, start to complain.

Look at what happened here! No one stood up to the rabbles and said, "Shut your mouth, respect Moses as our leader, and follow leadership, and furthermore, obey and accept the vision God has given him as our leader.

So what does God do?

He gives the people what they are asking for, not because He wants to, but because they need to be taught a lesson, even two in a row.

He gave them so much to eat it wasn't enough room for it all!

And there went forth a wind from the LORD, and brought quails from the sea, and let them fall by the camp, as it were a day's journey on this side, and as it were a day's journey on the other side, round about the camp, and as it were two cubits high upon the face of the earth. And the people stood up all that day, and all that night, and all the next day, and they gathered the quails: he that gathered least gathered ten homers: and they spread them all abroad for themselves round about the camp. And while the flesh was yet between their teeth, ere it was chewed, the wrath of the LORD was kindled against the people, and the LORD smote the people with a very great plague. And he called the name of that place Kibrothhattaavah: because there they buried the people that lusted (Numbers 11:31-34).

The people were exceptionally greedy. They desired death rather than life, and they received the desire of their hearts. The bread that comes down from heaven gives life. The Lord wanted to give them life, but because they still sought after death, He let them taste of it again, but only along with the bread of life, that they would hopefully realize the difference.

We must remain satisfied with God's blessings. In reality you can be satisfied. This is why Jesus came. He came to bring all men into a satisfying relationship with God. But that satisfying experience doesn't come automatically. It comes only when we meet God's conditions. And just what are His conditions? Basically, it is to repent of sin, to ask God to forgive us, and to personally ask Jesus Christ to come into our hearts by faith to be our Bread of life.

There is no short cut to a contented life. It comes through commitment to God, and Jesus Christ. But you can have it. The peace of God is actually a gift that God gives to every person who accepts the Saviour. You cannot earn this peace. It does not come through inheritance, or through our own efforts. It is the gift of God.

Chapter 18

Get Right Church and Let's Go Home

(Romans 6:1; 23 KJV)

What shall we say then? Shall we continue in sin, that grace may abound? For the wages of sin is death; but the gift of God is eternal life through Jesus Christ our Lord.

For some reason it is thought by people that a person can "live two lives." A person can be a Christian and continue to live as he or she always did before becoming a Christian. In fact, many seem to be living a life of double standards. Why is it that on the average 25% of the church membership will be in a worship service on any given Lord's Day? Why is it that 20% of a church membership gives 80% of the income in tithes and offering to support the Lord's Church? Why is it that even less than 20% are willing to serve their church family in some capacity?

It is impossible to live as the Lord wants; and to live a life of imperfection and impurities. Church members are bringing into the church their worldly ways of life. And therefore the church is no longer a sacred place, but has become another superficial place. The church has already declined in our generation, to the point that it is far from its main objective.

So, what can the church do to regain its spiritual momentum in our sacred place of worship? Well first and foremost. We must recognize who is it that interferes with the growth of the church; to cause it to become ineffective in right and righteousness.

I. The Interferences in the Church:

Interferences in the church mostly begin with the presence of Satan and his spiritual devices. Believe it or not, Satan is a real being and with the help of his demonic elms he inhabits real human beings. Satan never rests and is aggressive, *"Be sober, be vigilant; because your adversary the devil, as a roaring lion, walketh about, seeking whom he may devour"* (1st Peter 5:8).

Satan is behind every movement against Christianity using whatever and whomever he can to bring harm, destruction, division, discourse and an end to any Christian movement possible. The real fact to matter is! In order for him to set up post within the church, "Somebody has to bring him in."

Satan wants to hold on to every soul that he has. He does everything in his power to keep a lost person from hearing the gospel, and excuses to avoid Jesus.

Next, his purpose is to hamper believers to steal their joy, kill their faith, and destroy their destination. He would rather get a believer into sin than just about anything. Why is Satan so anxious in this area? Sin is the answer to this inquisitive question. Satan knows that, sin in the life of a believer, will bring about discouragement and depression.

He has great potential to destroy. Look around at our churches, who are dying, leaders who have fallen, and families which are dismantling their faith in God. Satan is having a buffet among God's redeemed, quite likely, because we do not see our enemy or his impact in our lives. When we do, we will resist him by exercising our faith.

When we realize that this is a spiritual warfare, recognize our enemy, and begin to ready ourselves for the battle, several things will begin to happen in our lives. Let me use the word Pray as an acrostic to help us.

P – Prayer- will become a greater source of strength. When we pray in faith we release the power of heaven.

R - Relationships - You are not alone. Someone is going through the same difficulties you are.

A - Action - The Bible will tell you the action to take when you are attacked.

Y - Yield - Always yield to the leadings of the Holy Spirit of God within you. If He's not there then the first yielding comes when you are saved. After that, He is a friend that sticks closer than a brother.

II. The Ineffectiveness of the Church:

Why does it seem as if the church has lost her appeal?

The Church now compromises with the world, not wanting to hurt any feelings, wanting to "blend" in and be "accepted" by all. Even those who are enemies to the Lord Jesus want a piece of the action!

The pastors who remain loyal and true to their calling are often rebuked and scolded by the Church members for being "too harsh in his preaching, too judgmental in his decisions, and too inexperienced in his education." They are told to preach less harshly because some members are more fragile than others. They purposely wear their feeling on their shoulders, especially when declining to follow leadership.

Dr. TCL Ward, professor at the Inner-Baptist Theological Seminary, Inc. once said, "The Church is the only place he knows that will hire a pastor, pay him, and refuse to let him fulfill his pastoral responsibilities."

In this day and age congregations are compromising with the world to gain its friendship and sadly, pastors are joining their congregations in compromise. In "worship" services, the music has been changed to fit the styles of the world, and services have become entertainment productions instead of times of worship. The pastoral sermons have been changed from God's Word to words that please and do not question nor upset.

True Christians need to understand and remember that anytime God's Word or the Gospel is preached. Somebody is going to be offended, for it is a stumbling block, a rock of offense to those who do not know nor love the Lord Jesus. When the gospel is preached, it is not a time for a community reunion or entertainment. It's a time to worship the Lord!

Worship, the word we use in English comes from an older word within the English history of its language, which means worth ship. This is the act of honoring God because he is worthy of it. So the word worship is directly related to the word worth. It's adoration, thanksgiving, prayers of all kinds, the offering of sacrifice and the making of vows. Worship embraces all of those things that are part of the history of the God's people and the history of the church.

III. Indifferences in the Church:

It is getting harder and harder for the preaching of God's Word to bring change in people. People today seem to have a "form" of godliness, but that's all. There is no power! There is no desire to do anything for the Lord. People don't want their "church life" interfering with their daily lives.

It is getting more difficult to get people "Christians" to take a stand for God and God's ways. People today don't necessarily oppose God's programs, nor do they make open, public statements in favor of things they do which are not Godly, but simply sit quietly, as unconcerned individuals, not willing to take a public stand for God.

IV. Introduction of the Church:

Jesus our "kurios" which means "Lord" or Master once said, that in the "last days" people would forsake Him, leave His church, and ignore their duties as Christians. Furthermore, our time looks like the time Jesus was speaking of! If you are a Christian, then you are also a church member, and it is far past time to stop "playing church" and get right with the Lord and return to what you are supposed to be doing for Him. Pastors and church leaders, your church is not some entertainment center. The church is a place of worship.

I invite you ask this question; who have we come to worship? When you start thinking about the fact that God is the sovereign Lord of all creation, you will not need to worry about when or where or how to engage in worship. You will just start praising God because of who God is.

Then I ask you to consider why we should worship God? What has the sovereign God done in my life that I should come before him with thanksgiving? If the Lord has saved you from the perils of your earlier life, worship him. If the Lord has saved you from the dangers and near-death encounters that have tracked you through the years you ought to worship.

Most importantly, however, if you know that the Lord went to the cross to pay the price for your sins, you ought to worship him. If you know that the Lord looked beyond your faults and saw your needs and washed your sins away with his precious cleansing blood, then you might not find it hard to say, "O come, let us worship and bow down, let us kneel before the Lord our maker." Worship is not about how to do it, or when to do it, or where to do it. Worship is about who is being worshipped and why that worship is deserved.

Chapter 19

⌇

Can I Have This Dance?

(2nd Samuel 6:16 KJV)

And as the ark of the LORD came into the city of David,
Michal Saul's daughter looked through a window and saw
King David leaping and dancing before the LORD, and she
despised him in her heart.

Let me open by asking an inquisitive question. "Do you really know how to dance?" I don't mean going to a night club, because most of us are too saved, too sanctified and too Holy Ghost filled to ever step foot in a night club.

May I ask "Do you ever dance at home when no one is around?" "Have you ever been in a great mood and one of your favorite songs comes on the radio, and as you are driving, before you know it your head is moving and your shoulders are swaying to the beat?" Here's a good one, "Have you ever practiced a dance you were going to attempt before you hit the party, but it didn't turn out right after you hit the dance floor?"

In our text there is some dancing going on. David danced before the Lord as the ark of God was being brought to Jerusalem. David and most of Israel were excited that the ark of the Lord had finally been brought home to Jerusalem. The ark of the Lord was significant because it represented the very presence of God on earth.

During the 40 years Israel spent wandering in the wilderness; the ark guided the pilgrims. Israel did not travel anywhere or do anything without the ark leading the way. The ark even led Israel in battle (Numbers 10:33, 35-36). One time Israel went into battle without the ark and attacked the Amalekites and Canaanites even though the ark stayed in the camp. The result was defeat in battle (Numbers 14:39-45).

The ark of the Lord had been away from the heart of Israel for twenty to forty years in this text. My God! That's a long time to be in a spiritual deficiency. David, a man after God's own heart knew the value of the ark of the Lord. David knew the value of God's presence. Shortly after David becomes king he goes to get the Ark of the Covenant.

Many years before this time, the Ark of the Covenant had been captured from Israel by the Philistines. The Ark was essentially a box which contained the golden pot of manna, Aaron's staff that budded, and the stone tablets of the covenant. And exclusively above the ark were two cherubim of the Glory overshadowing the Mercy Seat.

It contained items from their history with God. Again remember, that this sacred ark went with the Israelites. Wherever they traveled it was significantly a symbol of God's divine presence. No matter where the Israelites wandered. God was with right there. God independently would provide for them measures above their faith.

For about twenty to forty years under the rule of king Saul, Israel would be without the Ark as part of their national worship. Furthermore, the Ark of the Covenant abided at the house of Abinadab for safe-keeping.

David successfully conducted various military campaigns so that many of Israel's enemies would be defeated, dismantled, and destroyed. The Israelites didn't have to worry at this point about their enemies taking possession of the Ark of the Covenant ever again after it is returned.

David now decides to move the capital city from Shiloh to Jerusalem. He wanted to bring the Ark of the Covenant to his new capital city, which was to be not only the political center, but also the religious center of the nation. It has been a long time since the Israelites had a specific location that would serve as a center for worship.

David in return was accused of being a shrewd politician after he made this decision, but I think David does this out of the most sincere motives. David is portrayed as a man after God's own heart. David consistently shows that he legitimately worshipped God; and could not imagine being king without having God's blessing.

I. David's Mistake:

"And they set the ark of God upon a new cart, and brought it out of the house of Abinadab that was in Gibeah: and Uzzah and Ahio, the sons of Abinadab, drave the new cart" (2nd Samuel 6:3).

In (2nd Samuel chapter 6), we find the Ark of the Covenant resting at Abinadab house. David after authorizing the relocating of the ark, failed to instruct Abinadab and his two sons, on how to transition the ark to Jerusalem.

David allowed the ark of God to be carried upon a cart, and commanded that it be brought out of the house of Abinadab, which was on a hill. Uzzah and Ahio, sons of Abinadab, were driving the cart that was constructed by the Philistines, Israel's enemy.

On the Ark were rings which had poles through them. Men were to carry the Ark by using those poles. That was the prescribed method for carrying the Ark.

When Abinadab and his two sons were given the privilege of moving the Ark to Jerusalem, they formed a new idea and a new technology. They put the Ark on the cart so that the people would not be burdened. This sounds reasonable, but it was not what God instructed.

II. David's Music:

"And David and all the house of Israel played before the LORD on all manner of instruments made of fir wood, even on harps, and on psalteries, and on timbrels, and on cornets, and on cymbals" (2nd Samuel 6:5).

No doubt David could dance. Nobody had soul like that of David. Oh! David knew how to break it down. Just like some of you I must say!

David and all the house of Israel were dancing before the Lord with all their might, with songs and lyres, harps and tambourines, castanets and cymbals.

The procession of the Ark was accompanied with plenty of music, singing and even dancing. And no one danced more vigorously than David. This was a grand celebration. David definitely chose the right dance partner.

Wait one minute, (2nd Samuel 6:6-11) informs us of the death of Uzzah, one of the sons of Abinadab. As the procession begins, the oxen that were pulling the ark stumble and the ark begins to plunge to the ground. Uzzah naturally reaches out his hand to balance the ark and God struck him.

"The anger of the LORD was kindled against Uzzah; and God struck him there because he reached out his hand to the ark; and he died there beside the ark of God" (2nd Samuel 6:7).

When Uzzah died, they stopped the procession and waited for three months. David was disturbed and even angry with God over Uzzah's death.

Why did God's strike death upon Uzzah? Answer! The Ark has been in the house of his father for years. So, I assume homiletically that Uzzah and his brother had been taking care of the Ark. I can imagine him being angry about the Ark being relocated. He had come to a sense of ownership of the Ark. He had to protect the Ark, and in a sense protect God. Perhaps he also thought he could manage God.

Some of us try to put God in a box. We try to contain God. And we try to manage God. We don't want God to disturb our lives. So we put God where we want God to be. But! God is not so easily controlled.

III. David's Mindset:

Three months after this incident. David decided to leave the Ark of the Covenants at Obededom the Gittite house. After three months, the procession is resumed. We presume that this time, David does the procession right using the poles and humanity to carry the Ark. This time after every six steps, he stopped to make an offering to the Lord. He intended on making this procession right.

The Ark is brought into Jerusalem successfully. In verse 16, we get another character, *"As the ark of the Lord came into the city of David, Michal, daughter of Saul looked out of the window, and saw King David her husband leaping and dancing before the Lord; and she despised him in her heart."* That verse carries a lot of meaning.

When the parade is coming, what is Mical doing in the window? Why is she a spectator and not a participant?

Perhaps we are like Michal, carrying old bitterness and not able to bring ourselves to participate in the celebration of God. Are we spectators, and bystanders, critically looking at those who worship God in ways we do not approve?

Perhaps we are like Uzzah thinking, God is in our box? Do we think we control God? Are we the kind of people who try to put a hand on God? If so, the Bible's message for us is, "Beware of God."

Perhaps we are like David. A person who was genuine who trusted God and his reflexes? He was not one to manipulate God or control God. He had a reason to dance. He was not a spectator; he had a reason to dance. He was a part of the celebration, worshipping God with all his heart and might. He let his emotions go. God loved David because he was a man after His own heart.

David has been celebrating by dancing and he's almost literally out of his clothing except his ephod by this point. Michal sees her husband. She's upset that he is behaving in this manner.

I truly believe that David and Michal had a little argument about this incident. Michal confronts David concerning his conduct by suggesting. David did this to draw attention of those around him, especially the handmaids (2nd Samuel 6:20).

In the final paragraph, the Ark is brought into the temple. There are offerings, and David gives to everyone a cake of bread, a portion of meat, and a cake of raisins, then all the people went back to their homes.

That's the story. Now let's try to draw a lesson from the main character David. His story holds center place in this story. The big question is, "Why did David dance?" He danced before the Ark, reckless and joyful. David was the kind of person who responded with his heart and he trusted his reactions. He went with his instincts and chose the right dance partner.

Chapter 20

⚛

They Gathered At the Cross

(Luke 23:33-37 KJV)

And when they were come to the place, which is called Calvary, there they crucified him, and the malefactors, one on the right hand, and the other on the left. Then said Jesus, Father, forgive them; for they know not what they do. And they parted his raiment, and cast lots. And the people stood beholding. And the rulers also with them derided him, saying, He saved others; let him save himself, if he be Christ, the chosen of God. And the soldiers also mocked him, coming to him, and offering him vinegar, And saying, If thou be the king of the Jews, save thyself.

There have been many world disasters and tragedies, such as war, disease, floods, winds, and earthquakes that have killed hundreds of people and rendered millions homeless.

However there is one tragedy that outweighs all world tragedies put together. This transpired over 2,000 years ago. Whereas, the Son of God hung six hours on the cross, on a hill called Calvary; also known as Golgotha or the Place of the Skull.

While hanging on the cross, Jesus our kinsman redeemer authorized the sun to hide its face. He made the earth stagger like a drunken man. He made the mountains trembled as if they were horrified. He allowed the dead to rise from their graves, and caused the great veil of the temple to split from top to bottom.

This was the world's greatest tragedy ever to occur. The question is often asked, "Who crucified Jesus?" Have you ever wondered if it was the Romans who Mark would write to? Or was it Pilate the governor of Rome who was responsible?

What about the Jews who Matthew would write to? Did the Jews crucify Jesus? The disciples were Jews. The apostles were Jews. John, the beloved, was a Jew. John the Baptist was a Jew. Peter, who preached the great Pentecost sermon, was a Jew. The nearest and dearest to the heart of Jesus were all Jews.

Therefore the center of the question is not who; but what crucified Jesus? Whatever drove Jesus to Calvary is still active and busy today for Jesus is still being crucified each and every day. There were crowds of people around the three crosses, who made up of different kinds of people. Try for a moment to locate your-self in this crowd, for each of us belongs to one of these different groups of people that were at the cross.

The first crowd we observe that gathered at the cross was:

I. Those who Disrespected Jesus while on the Cross:

They watched Him while on the cross. It was a celebration for them to watch Jesus suffer. There were some in the crowd who openly opposed Jesus and made havoc of him. There were some who actually hated Jesus called the Sanhedrin council. The Sanhedrin council showed such disrespect of His ability to expose their sins and redefine their laws.

He demolished their religious views and had shown them up for what they really were. They were blind, guilty, deceptive, dishonest and hypocritical.

I believe with my sanctified imagination that the meat market man was in the crowd, whom Jesus authorized the devils to enter into his swine; causing them to drown themselves in the sea. This man lost ten-thousand hams. He loss plenty of breakfast bacon, hog head cheese, four thousand pickled pigs' feet, hog maws, pork sausages, hot links, pork tenderloins, and Chitlins.

The meat market man wouldn't have missed this event to save his life. So many were there in the crowd who opposed Jesus! Many groups in the crowd are duplicated today. The divine spotlight is on every dishonest business person, every crooked politician, every publisher who indulges himself in printed impurities, promoter of sexual literature, movies and television programs, including violators of judicial and morals laws.

These types of individuals dislike preachers, churches, and true Christians. They are quick to find some church scandal or some church members fault.

There are only two sides in the eyes of God. There's the side of the Saviour and the side of Satan. If one has not believed in Jesus that person is in that disrespectful crowd.

The second crowd we observe that gathered at the cross was:

II. Those who Deserted Jesus while on the Cross:

There were those who gathered around the crosses who had no feelings for anybody on those crosses, especially the one called Jesus.

In fact, every church, denomination, and community has these kinds of people. These are the church members who have moved away; taking everything with them except their church membership.

These are those who don't really care about the work of Jesus. Their children grow up in a place where the name of Jesus is obsolete. In the home there's not much prayer, and not one individual has a mindset to ever witness to anyone. They give very little if anything monetarily in support of the ministry of the church. They call themselves "Christians" when asked by someone, but would God call them one of His disciples? They have deserted Jesus!

- Where was Peter? He was nowhere to be found in the crowd! He Deserted Jesus. As a matter of fact it was Simon Peter who informed Jesus, that he would die in His place but where is he?

- Where was Joseph? He was nowhere to be found in the crowd. He also deserted Jesus! Theologians suggest that Joseph was deceased. But if that was the case, Jesus would have raised Joseph up! So he would be at His crucifixion.

They deserted Jesus! Ask yourself, "When was the last time you deserted Jesus?"

The third crowd we observe that gathered at the cross was:

III. Those who Desired Jesus while on the Cross:

In small numbers, some of the Lord's close friends were there because they loved Jesus enough to share the shame, and hate of the crowd. They shared Jesus agony and disappointments. They lingered there until Jesus sent them away.

"Now there stood by the cross of Jesus his mother, and his mother's sister, Mary the wife of Cleophas, and Mary Magdalene. When Jesus therefore saw his mother, and the disciple standing by, whom he loved, he saith unto his mother, Woman, behold thy son! Then saith he to the disciple, Behold thy mother! And from that hour that disciple took her unto his own home" (John 19:25-27).

Since Jesus was the oldest son. It was His responsibility to always see that His mother was cared for. This was a Jewish custom and also part of honoring one's parents in accordance with the commandment.

As Jesus knew that His death was near, though He was agonizing in severe pain, knowing that He was about to make the ultimate sacrifice according to God's plan; His last physical concern was to make provisions for His mother, whom He deeply respected and dearly loved.

The church group is still small today. There are so few among the millions on church rolls who would go with Jesus all the way to Calvary. In church memberships there are groups who may be counted true to Jesus and His Gospel. What would become of the Church if not for these few?

What crowd would you have involved yourself? Jesus is only interested in those who are among the desired crowd.

Chapter 21

‿✿‿

Discovering Our Assigned Roles

(Romans 12:1-4 KJV)

I beseech you therefore, brethren, by the mercies of God, that ye present your bodies a living sacrifice, holy, acceptable unto God, which is your reasonable service. And be not conformed to this world: but be ye transformed by the renewing of your mind, that ye may prove what is that good, and acceptable, and perfect, will of God. For I say, through the grace given unto me, to every man that is among you, not to think of himself more highly than he ought to think; but to think soberly, according as God hath dealt to every man the measure of faith. For as we have many members in one body, and all members have not the same office:

The church is the body of Christ. *"And hath put all things under his feet, and gave him to be the head over all things to the church, which is his body, the fullness of him that filleth all in all"* (Ephesians 1:22-23). Almost every time the church is spoken of as a body in the New Testament, reference is made to the functional aspect of the church. In these verses Paul speaks of the fullness of the body and how Christ fills the church. The church is a living organism Christ fills to function on his behalf. Here we see the functional aspect of the body of Christ.

In the text Paul is concerned about the functional aspect of the body. The body of Christ has many members functioning in various ways. Therefore, obviously each member of the body has a special function to fill.

In the book of Romans, Paul has been talking about what God has done for us in salvaging our lives. Now he turns to the practical aspect of Christianity giving us insight as to how we are to function in Christ. How do we begin to fill our God given role as members of the body? Paul begins answering this question in this chapter.

The church main objective should be that of **peace**, **perfection**, **persistence** and **perseverance**.

I. The Body must be Wholly Dedicated:

"I beseech you therefore, brethren, by the mercies of God, that ye present your bodies a living sacrifice, holy, acceptable unto God, which is your reasonable service. And be not conformed to this world: but be ye transformed by the renewing of your mind, that ye may prove what is that good, and acceptable, and perfect, will of God" (Romans 12:1-2).

A few years ago I was into cameras and during that time most of the flashes for cameras were bought separately. The question you wanted answered before you bought a particular flash was, "Is the flash unit dedicated to my particular brand of camera?" If the flash wasn't dedicated it would either not function at all or would not be fully functional. A dedicated flash was one made to fit your particular brand of camera in a fully functional mode. It was compatible to all the features the body of your camera offered. If the flash was a dedicated flash it formed one fully operational unit, although it was made up of two distinct pieces.

In Romans Chapter 12, Paul is concerned about members of Christ being fully dedicated to Christ body in a fully functional mode. The body of Christ is made up of many parts, which are designed to work in sync with every other part. To be fully functional as the body of Christ, we must get in sync with Christ as we renew our minds to transform our lives to be like Christ. If we are out of sync with the body of Christ; we must remember there is a place for each of us in the body, where we can be operative fully functional.

"But now hath God set the members every one of them in the body, as it hath pleased him" (1 Corinthians 12:18). God has made a place for each member of the body to be fully functional and dedicated. This is God's way of telling us the body of Christ needs each member.

The way we get in sync with Christ body is to offer our bodies as a living sacrifice to God. We must remember God has assigned each of us a place in the body of Christ. We must offer ourselves as a living sacrifice when we dedicate ourselves to fill the role God has assigned us.

II. The Body must be Workably Descriptive:

"For as we have many members in one body, and all members have not the same office: So we, being many, are one body in Christ, and every one members one of another. Having then gifts differing according to the grace that is given to us, whether prophecy, let us prophesy according to the proportion of faith; Or ministry, let us wait on our ministering: or he that teacheth, on teaching; Or he that exhorteth, on exhortation: he that giveth, let him do it with simplicity; he that ruleth, with diligence; he that sheweth mercy, with cheerfulness" (Romans 12:4-8).

We cannot all fill the same role. However, we can fill the role God has given us. The great Historian, Dr. G.W. Odom, Professor of the Inter-Baptist Theological Seminary, Inc. once said, "Before you are put over something, you first must learn how to be under something" case closed!

III. The Body must be Willfully Determined:

For I say, through the grace given unto me, to every man that is among you, not to think of himself more highly than he ought to think; but to think soberly, according as God hath dealt to every man the measure of faith (Romans 12:3).

To function properly, we must think soberly:

I think most of us know what it means to be sober; it is to think rationally. One of the hindrances to thinking rationally is to get an inflated view of one's self. All of us know what happens when others get an inflated view of themselves. It is the same thing that happens to you when you get an inflated view of yourself.

What if you woke up one morning with your big toes sticking out of your eye sockets and your eyeballs were attached to where your big toes once were? If they could talk, you would ask them what they thought they were doing, only to discover that sometime during the night your eye balls and big toes had decided to exchange locations.

Try to imagine how you would function if this occurred. First of all you have been awakened because of this excruciating pain coming from where your big toes use to be. You know how tender the eyeballs are! Well the eyeball has a sheet wrapped around it and it is hurting. So you blink your eyelid to try to correct the problem but the eyelid decided to stay put over the eye socket, and it can no longer protect the eye. So when you blink your eyelid to relieve the pain of the eyeball; one big toenail has a hangnail and it really hurts every time you blink, it feels like you have a log in your eye.

So as you kick your foot to get the sheet off the eyeball to relieve the pain, it just intensifies. So you jump out of bed and black your eyes as they hit the floor trying to be your big toes. It hurts so bad you try to keep your eyeballs from touching the floor as you walk and you fall flat on your face and stump both of your big toes, which are sticking out of your eye sockets.

You see your big toes are responsible for eighty percent of your balance when you walk. So you manage to get up off the floor, but you try to walk on your heels to keep the pressure off your blackened eyeballs. As you swing your right foot around the end of the bed, trying not to stump your eye on the end of the bed, you swing your foot out a little too far and bust your eye on the corner of the dresser, because your big toes can't see where your eyes are going.

So you sit down and have a talk with your eyeballs and your big toes to instruct them to get back in their assigned roles, but both are adamant about staying where they are. Their refusal to function in their assigned roles affects the whole body's ability to function properly.

Sometimes one of the hardest things to do is to get someone out of a position they have coveted but are not qualified to fill. Allowing them to stay there makes the body ineffective, and getting them out disrupts the whole body for it is a matter of major surgery.

Whatever the position God is calling each of us to fulfill is not an inferior position. It is not always easy to figure out how God wants you to function or what part you are supposed to play. We usually discover where God wants us by trial and error.

If you fill your role with the help of the Holy Spirit, realizing God is standing beside you, ready to deliver you from the mouth of the lion; then you can step out on God's power to accomplish his will in and through you. If you are worried about filling God's assigned role, remember you have the Holy Spirit who lives in you to strengthen you, and remember "The Lord is at your side."

Chapter 22

⁓

Being Sure In a Strange World

(Psalm 119:11 KJV)

Thy word have I hid in mine heart, that I might not sin against thee.

A young man from a wealthy family was about to graduate from high school. It was a custom in their affluent community for parents to give their graduating children a new car. The boy and his dad had spent weeks visiting one dealership after another. The week before graduation they found the perfect car. The boy was certain it would be in the driveway on graduation night.

However, on the eve of his graduation his father handed him a small package wrapped in colorful paper. The Father said the package contained the most valuable gift. Certainly it was a bible. The boy was so angry that he threw the bible down, and stormed out of the house. He and his father never saw each other again.

Several years later the news of the father's death finally brought the son home again. Following the funeral he sat alone one evening, going through his father's possessions that he was to inherit. When he came across the bible his dad had given him. He was overwhelmed by grief; he brushed away the dust and cracked it open for the first time. He discovered a cashier's check dated the day of his high school graduation, as it fell into his lap. The exact amount of the car they had chosen together was written into this cashier's check. The gift had been there all along but he had turned it away.

The most valuable gift our Father has given us is His Word. The only way we can learn to live with all of the pressure, problems, and perplexities of life is to learn how to live in the Word of God. We are to preach and spread the Word in a strange world.

To be sure of God's word in a strange world you must remember his word is:

- Wonderful in its inspiration.
- Wonderful in its unification.
- Wonderful in its translation.
- Wonderful in its preservation.
- Wonderful in its salvation.
- Wonderful in its sanctification.
- Wonderful in its consummation.

It attracts the simple minds and confounds the deepest thinkers. It is always up to date and meets today's needs. It is so complete in its coverage of all human conditions that it's sometimes incomprehensible.

When we live by His Word we will:

- Recognize its divine authority and bow to it.
- Own its glorious supremacy and obey it.
- Confess it blessed and rejoice in it.
- Cling to its holy integrity and testify to it.
- Cherish its precious truths and feed on it.
- Know its blessed truth and walk in the light of it.

The only way we can learn to survive and meet the demands of this day is to learn how to live in the word.

What do you think about the bible?

- When you look at it, it's not expensive china that you can't touch and have to handle with caution.
- We don't write on it "fragile do not break" it was made to be handled.
- We don't put it on a shelf to collect dust and say isn't that a beautiful bible.

The word is to be **Examined**, **Experienced**, and **Expressed**. That's the way the Word really comes alive!

I. Be Sure to Examine the Word:

When you examine the sureness of God's Word for yourself you'll discover that what God has given to us is a Gift. A whole lot of people are drowning in damnation because of denying the gift of God's Word.

In order to survive in this world, you must examine the Word before you can effectively face a world of opposition. You must study God's Word for nourishment of your spiritual being. You should study it thoroughly in a digestible manner (see Psalm 34:8).

The Word of God is our survival manual, and if you live right according to it's predestine oracles, you'll soar to boundaries unimaginable. Whenever you decide to let down your landing gear of spiritual educational preparation; and glean from your spiritual leaders a prioritized presentation of salvation; remember to personally examine God's Word as the first principle of your life.

II. Be Sure to Experience the Word:

Hide His Word in your heart and when you need Him the most you'll recognize Him as being your safe haven. He'll bring you out of some stupendous situations. I dare you to try Him by His Word!

God want us to hide His Word in our hearts just as David does so in (Psalm 119:11), which reads, "Thy *word have I hid in mine heart, that I might not sin against thee.*"

So how can you do the same? Well, here are three ways. First, you need to hear God's Word, afterwards, receive it, and then meditate on it.

There's hymn you should always remember called:

"In Times Like These"

(Verse 1)
In times like these you need a Savior
In times like these you need an anchor
Be very sure, be very sure
Your anchor holds and grips the Solid Rock

(Refrain)
This Rock is Jesus, Yes He's the One
This Rock is Jesus, the only One
Be very sure, be very sure
Your anchor holds and grips the Solid Rock

(Verse 2)
In times like these you need the Bible
In times like these O be not idle
Be very sure, be very sure
Your anchor holds and grips the Solid Rock

(Verse 3)
In times like these I have a Savior
In times like these I have an anchor
I'm very sure, I'm very sure
My anchor holds and grips the Solid Rock

III. Be Sure to Express the Word:

When you have experienced God's Word, you can't keep Him a secret. You will have no problem telling others what the Lord has done for you. Brag on Him! The reason you can brag on Him is because you refuse to keep Him a secret.

There is a rising challenge for the believers today to present the Word in a manner that is no secret; and relevant to those we are attempting to reach without compromising truth of the Word. In order to effectively reach a post modern world, the church must address the culture in which we live and learn how to effectively communicate the timeless message of God in a manner in which they can receive.

Chapter 23

⚜

You Are Not the Father

(Matthew 1:19-20 KJV)

Then Joseph her husband, being a just man, and not willing to make her a public example, was minded to put her away privily. But while he thought on these things, behold, the angel of the LORD appeared unto him in a dream, saying, Joseph, thou son of David, fear not to take unto thee Mary thy wife: for that which is conceived in her is of the Holy Ghost.

I am a number one fan of the Maury Show. Sometime ago as I was viewing the show, there was a young lady named Telia on the show; she was extremely excited about DNA testing a guy named Dion to determine if he'd be proven to be her child's biological father. Dion, assured Maury that surely he was not the father, and that Maury would not only be testing him as the eleventh person; but it will be a miracle if he ever found the biological father.

Telia assured Maury out of all the other ten guys he invited to the show. This time she has the right one! Before Maury could even read the results, she obnoxiously disrespected Dion to the point, she mentioned that she told the whole world that Dion was the father, and that it was time for him to step up to the plate and accept his responsibility.

Maury received the test results and said to him, "Dion when it comes to Shardea. Mr. Dion you are not the father!" With much excitement,

Dion danced off the stage in victory, and Telia dashed off the stage and vanished.

In the case of the child in our text, the bible gives no name of that angel that appeared unto Joseph, and informed him that he was not the father! The text acknowledges this angel as the Angel of the Lord. The words, "Angel of the Lord" in research always points back to Christ and his personage.

Here is the Angel of the Lord (Jesus) appearing in a dream to Joseph, while at the same time. He's developing in the womb of Mary. What a God!

Here is a baby, lying in Mary's womb as a cradle, while at the same time. He's sitting in the chair of sovereignty in Heaven. What a God!

Here is a baby in the womb of Mary, younger than both Joseph and Mary, but yet older than time. What a God!

What disturbing news to Brother Joseph, "Joseph when it comes to baby Jesus! You are not the father!"

When I exegeses this chapter I see:

I. The Stunting Disappointment:

Mary and Joseph were betrothed to one another. This was the ancient Hebrew engagement period and it was as binding as a marriage. Surely, they were excited about their future together as husband and wife.

A marriage was considered legal after the betrothing period. The woman was the man's wife even though she continued to live at her own family home, usually for about a year. That is why a formal certificate of divorce was required to break the vows. That's also why a woman was considered a widow if the man died before she was taken into his home.

We are told, "Mary was pledged to be married to Joseph." This means Joseph and Mary had already gone through the first step of marriage and were considered husband and wife. That's why Joseph is identified as "her husband" (Matthew 1:19).

In this light consider the fact that Mary "was found to be with child" (Matthew 1:18). At this point Joseph knew only one thing about the child inside Mary. What a stunting disappointment! Joseph knew about the child. That he was not the father. Joseph was not going to broadcast this situation. This could only mean that Mary had been sleeping around. Another man had slept with his wife! As far as Joseph was concerned; he could not and would not take Mary into his home.

II. The Sobering Deliberation:

In the midst of this stunting disappointment; Joseph's true self is revealed. We are told that he was a "just" man. This simply means that he was blameless under the Law and that he walked by faith in the Lord. He was a man of God before these events befell him; and what he was in his heart came to surface in his trials.

Joseph was also a merciful, caring, and compassionate man. He did not want to humiliate Mary. He did not want to shame her in front of the entire world. He did not want to publicly accuse her of a serious sin. He did not want to subject her to a district trial. He did not want her to be executed for her sin according to (Deuteronomy 22:20-21). So he decided to divorce Mary quietly.

III. The Satisfying Declaration:

As these thoughts troubled the mind of Joseph; the Lord sent an angel to speak to him in a dream. The angel brought Joseph a word of **Explanation, Exaltation,** and **Exhilaration.** Joseph was made to understand the origin of the child his bride carried. He was made to understand that his dream; turned into a nightmare in his heart and mind.

Joseph is given details of a miracle that much of the world still has not grasped. God entered this world through the womb of a Jewish virgin. Joseph is told that Mary will have a son, and that this son is to be named Jesus. He is also told that this son will be the Savior of the Jews. That is quite a revelation! Concisely, Joseph is made aware that this child is no ordinary baby. In fact, he is the Son of God. His name will reflect that because the name Jesus means *"Jehovah is Salvation."*

IV. The Soothing Dedication:

As soon as Joseph understands what is happening in his life. He reacts in faith. He goes and takes Mary into his home and his heart as his wife. Here's a response of pure faith. He still does not know how things will work out, but he knows that God is working. And that is enough for Joseph. Joseph's decision must have shocked the whole community. Everyone probably assumed that Joseph and Mary had not been able to wait for the wedding. He was willing to bear the shame of Mary's pregnancy because he knew it was the work of God.

Joseph waited patiently until Mary gave birth to her son. No doubt, Joseph cared for the expectant mother as best he could. When the time came and the baby was born. Joseph did the job of the father. He named the boy Jesus as commanded.

The child was required to be named by the Father (Luke 1:63). Joseph is saying that he is willing to embrace the plan of God for his life, even though he does not fully understand it. He is willing to raise this child as his own, even though he knows he's not the father.

Chapter 24

✑

Top Priority of Authentic Worship

(John 4:24 KJV)

God is a Spirit: and they that worship him must worship him
in spirit and in truth.

The worshiping of God is a matter of great importance and great significance, as it is clearly seen in God's word. The word "worship" is found 119 times in the entire Bible.

So, what is worship? In scripture the word "worship" is **Proskuneo –** (**pros-koo-neh'-o**) which means in simplicity: *To kiss ones hand is a token of reverence.*

In studying the custom and manners among the Orientals, especially the Persians, they had to fall upon their knees, and touch the ground with the forehead as an expression of profound reverence.

In the Old Testament and New Testament, a few forms of true worship consisted of dressing out in sack cloth and ashes, kneeling, and lying prostrate before the Lord to express respect and or to make supplication. This was considered true worship between dust and divinity, creature and creator, finite and infinite.

God authorizes six items of worship:

- Singing (1 Cor. 14:15).
- Praying (Acts 2:42).
- Preaching (Acts 20:7).
- Lord's Supper (1 Cor. 11:20-30).
- Baptism (Matthew 28:19).
- Giving (1 Cor. 16:1-2).

All acts of worship must be carried out as God has commanded.

However sadly, I have discovered that many people evidently do not enjoy true authentic worship for several reasons.

- They are late in arriving to worship.
- They leave early before the conclusion of the worship.
- They seem disinterested while in worship and can't wait until it's over.

Many church services start extremely cold and calloused. Satan has become the coroner. So when the clock hand, strikes its allocated curfew in the worship. The church gives up her dead.

Jesus castigated the woman in the text who perceived Him to be a prophet. He exposed this Samaritan woman sins in a way that a man had never done before. This woman knew she had to make peace with God for her sins. She didn't have a husband of her own. She seems to be a type of street woman, who made the worship of God so narrow by explaining to Jesus that when the Samaritans worshiped God, it was always in the mountain where their forefathers worshiped. Jesus then explains to this woman. She can't limit God just to the mountain and Jerusalem.

God is omnipresent. He's every where all at the same time. The worship of God should be involved in everything we do every day. We are to honor

Him, glorify Him, and praise Him in all things. We must worship God "*in spirit and in truth*." Furthermore, in the Spirit of Christ we must worship Him.

Our love must be love that we see reflected in Christ. What did He do? How did He reveal His love? Was it in coming down for His own reward?

Christ in his self existence condescended Himself, and gave up His throne. He condescended Himself to be conceived in the womb, and birthed with a sinless nature. He condescended Himself to eat with publicans and sinners. He condescended Himself to die for sinners like us. He condescended and humbled Himself to fulfill our needs. That's the Spirit of Christ; a spirit that every believer should posses.

Let's take a closer look at the Observance of Our Worship:

I. The Observance of Our Worship:

But the hour cometh, and now is, when the true worshippers shall worship the Father in spirit and in truth: for the Father seeketh such to worship him (John 4:23).

Jesus is saying "a time is coming," "*the true worshipers will worship the Father in spirit and truth*" (4:23), there will no longer be any Temple, either in Jerusalem or Samaria. The same truth is set forth in the Book of Revelation, "*And I saw no temple therein: for the Lord God Almighty and the Lamb are the temple of it*" (Revelation 21:22). With the coming of the Holy Spirit on the day of Pentecost, one witnesses the new concept of "*in Spirit and truth*." Jesus, in his conversation with the woman of Samaria, tells how this eschatological time and its worship of God are to be understood.

When we come to worship we must be participants and not spectators, many "worshippers" come to Church services filled with worldliness. Their minds and hearts are preoccupied with things of the world rather than with the Lord God and their worship of Him.

In fact, coming to church infected with the world virus of hostile attitudes, and fault finding motive will rob ones spiritual worship benefits and bring bitterness into the soul.

In true worship we must remember we are not the main attraction. God should be the main attraction, and our aim then should be to please God, and never worry about how strange men may take inventory of our worship.

However, some say, "I just don't get anything out of worship. The pastor just seems to be preaching the same old antique messages that we've been hearing for years."

This type of demonic, derogative, depressing, delineative statement is a false concept of authentic worship. If you are not getting anything out of worship; it's because you're not putting enough into it. Satan has stolen your main focus.

The problem with the church these days is too much lip service, and not enough worshiping service. The Holy Scriptures gives a direct definitive endorsement to this profound statement.

"This people honoureth Me with their lips, but their heart is far from Me. Howbeit in vain do they worship Me"(Matthew 15:8).

A believer who has fallen out of the will of God cannot worship God in spirit and truth. Their heart has caused them to distance themselves from the Lord God, and the only thing they are offering is lip services.

A person can be sincere, generous, zealous, devout and regular in church attendance. Yet be no more effective of worshipping the Lord God; than a person without a tongue singing in the church choir.

Jesus as God deserves to be worshiped. He has been worshiped as God from his first minutes on the earth. Let's trace the ways that Jesus was worshiped as described in the Gospel eyewitness accounts of His life.

The wise men worshiped Him from the moment He was born:

When they saw the star, they rejoiced with exceeding great joy. And when they were come into the house, they saw the young child with Mary his mother, and fell down, and worshipped him: and when they had opened their treasures, they presented unto him gifts; gold, and frankincense and myrrh. And being warned of God in a dream that they should not return to Herod, they departed into their own country another way (Matthew 2:10-12).

The leper worshiped Him at his healing:

And, behold, there came a leper and worshipped him, saying, "Lord, if thou wilt, thou canst make me clean" (Matthew 8:2).

The synagogue ruler worshiped Him:

While he spake these things unto them, behold, there came a certain ruler, and worshipped him, saying, "My daughter is even now dead: but come and lay thy hand upon her, and she shall live." And Jesus arose, and followed him, and so did his disciples (Matthew 9:18-19).

The disciples worshiped Him in the boat:

And when they were come into the ship, the wind ceased. Then they that were in the ship came and worshipped him, saying, "Of a truth thou art the Son of God" (Matthew 14:32-33).

The Canaanite woman worshiped Him:

Then came she and worshipped him, saying, "Lord, help me." But he answered and said, "It is not meet to take the children's bread, and to cast it to dogs" (Matthew 15:25-26).

The mother of James and John worshipped Him:

Then came to him the mother of Zebedees children with her sons, worshipping him, and desiring a certain thing of him. And he said unto her, "What wilt thou?" She saith unto him, "Grant that these my two sons may sit, the one on thy right hand, and the other on the left, in thy kingdom" (Matthew 20:20-21).

The blind man worshiped Him at his healing:

Jesus heard that they had cast him out; and when he had found him, he said unto him, "Dost thou believe on the Son of God?" He answered and said, "Who is he, Lord, that I might believe on him?" And Jesus said unto him, "Thou hast both seen him, and it is he that talketh with thee." And he said, "Lord, I believe. And he worshipped him" (John 9:35-38).

The women worshiped Him at the empty tomb:

And they departed quickly from the sepulchre with fear and great joy; and did run to bring his disciples word. And as they went to tell his disciples, behold, Jesus met them, saying, "All hail." And they came and held him by the feet, and worshipped him. Then said Jesus unto them, "Be not afraid: go tell my brethren that they go into Galilee, and there shall they see me" (Matthew 28:8-10).

The disciples worshiped Him at the Ascension:

Then the eleven disciples went away into Galilee, into a mountain where Jesus had appointed them. And when they saw him, they worshipped him: but some doubted (Matthew 28:16-17).

Let's take a closer look at the Object of Our Worship:

II. The Object of Our Worship:

God is a Spirit: and they that worship him must worship him in spirit and in truth (John 4:24).

The place of worship is not what's important! What is important is the object of our worship.

God is seriously concerned about how we worship Him. He gives specific commands about how He wants to be glorified, according to His standards and not our own standards. There is no choice in the matter of worship given to people; but one way to worship God.

Those who have been born again and regenerated, and who are resting upon the atoning sacrificial work of the Lord Jesus Christ can't help but to worship the Lord God. There are no options. It's an opportunity of continuance to praise Him. Let's Worship Him!

Chapter 25

_♈_

God's Super Bowl Game

(Proverbs 15:3 KJV)

The eyes of the LORD are in every place, beholding the evil and the good.

The Super Bowl is a football game played each year to determine the championship of the National Football League. The game is played by two teams of eleven players each on a rectangular, 100-yard-long field with goal lines and goal posts. The object of the game is to gain possession of the ball and advance it in running or passing plays across the opponent's goal line or kick it through the air between the opponent's goal posts.

The Super Bowl reminds me of the world in which we reside.

Amazingly, it's as if God is watching the Super Bowl Game. He is watching over and protecting his Saints. He's watching how we are seceding in the game of life.

God is interested in three areas of our lives:

- The **Uniformity** of the Saints.
- The **Uniqueness** of the Saints.
- The **Undivided** attention of the Saints.

I. The Uniformity of the Saints:

In order to overcome the strategic strategy of Satan's game. The Saints must work together knowing that it's just not a one man or woman show. What's wrong with the church of the 21st century? There's too much show, and self on the spiritual fields of warfare. This has caused the Saints blessings to be intercepted.

Have you ever been on the verge of working out a problem and trouble was about to enter out the back door, and the devil start climbing through the windows or out the cabinets? To win against the arch enemy it's imperative that the Saints work and worship together against his demonic agenda. The next time Satan tries to climb into your spiritual window. Execute the offensive move by calling on the Father, Son and Holy Ghost.

The word uniformity is derived from the word unify. In order to win the game of life; Saints must unify themselves with the will of God, and love Him perfectly.

The more one unites his will with the divine will. The greater will be his love of God. Unity is essential to the followers of Jesus. It is not just friendliness or a togetherness, but perfect oneness. It's being together as one. Real Saints are those who know how to plant themselves; in the garden of unity and bloom pedals of strength as its outcome. In other words, Christians should give themselves completely to each other, just as do the persons of the Trinity. The church as the body of Christ should reveal the love and unity of God.

II. The Uniqueness of the Saints:

The authenticity of real Saints is unique in many ways. Each of them dress out in the same attire, and each team player stands out in the crowd, but when it comes to their uniqueness, all of them are assigned a certain number. They are assigned a specific number to help win the game.

Each team must have an **offensive**, and a **defensive side** to play the game.

The offense in football is the team that begins a play from scrimmage in possession of the ball. A play usually begins when the quarterback, who takes a snap from the center, and then either hands off the ball to a running or tail back, or passes to a receiver or a back, or runs the ball himself, or spikes the ball or takes a knee.

The defensive team is the team that begins the play from scrimmage, who's not in possession of the ball. The object of the defensive team is to prevent the other team from scoring. The sign that the defensive goal has been accomplished is recovering the possession of the football before the offensive team scores, which usually involves the offensive team punting the ball on fourth down. Other possibilities include having the ball turned over on the downs, getting an interception or recovering a fumble.

Pay close attention! It's as if when it comes to the finite, "God is watching the Super Bowl Game." God represents the Center who puts the ball (nails), in Jesus' hand our Quarter Back, who ran the ball all the way to Calvary's Hill and scored a touchdown. He took the victory from Satan. The defensive line of death, and ended his deadly scheme.

III. The Undivided Attention of the Saints:

To win the game you must be tested *"**Somebody Gotta Win and Somebody Gotta Loose**"* So, that's why there's a coach appointed to every team. The coach is responsible for teaching the strategy on how to win the game. He has to remind you that he's the one in charge! You must not only listen but also hear him demonstrate the plays on how to win the game. Before the game in the locker room, he makes the team dress out. After dressing out, he meets and reminds the team to keep the focus on the field, and let nothing distract you!

Jesus is the Coach of the Saints team who taught us how to deal with our opponent the adversary. *"These things I have spoken unto you, that in me ye might have peace. In the world ye shall have tribulation: but be of good cheer; I have overcome the world"* (John 16:33).

Every Saint should put on the Christian uniform. As expressed in God's inspired Word.

"Finally, my brethren, be strong in the Lord, and in the power of his might. Put on the whole armour of God, that ye may be able to stand against the wiles of the devil. For we wrestle not against flesh and blood, but against principalities, against powers, against the rulers of the darkness of this world, against spiritual wickedness in high places. Wherefore take unto you the whole armour of God, that ye may be able to withstand in the evil day, and having done all, to stand. Stand therefore, having your loins girt about with truth, and having on the breastplate of righteousness; And your feet shod with the preparation of the gospel of peace; Above all, taking the shield of faith, wherewith ye shall be able to quench all the fiery darts of the wicked. And take the helmet of salvation, and the sword of the Spirit, which is the word of God:" (Ephesians 6:10-17).

We all face spiritual battles, although we might not recognize them as such. The enemy of our soul is trying to trip us up in our spiritual walk, and trying to keep others blinded from accepting Christ. When we go forward to work in God's kingdom, we must be willing to meet physical opposition as well as spiritual opposition. We are both body and spirit. We may keep our body fit and ready but how healthy is our spirit? There will be spiritual battles ahead, and Paul is exhorting us to put on spiritual armor to withstand the devil and to stand firm for Christ.

In the conclusion of God's Super Bowl Game; Jesus will be standing at the door waiting for you to show and give an account of your deeds during the game. Will you be prepared to acclaim, *"**We won the Super Bowl Game?**"*

Contact Information:

Dr. Richie Bell, Jr.
Pilgrim Travelers' Missionary Baptist Church
604 Harrison Street
Shreveport, Louisiana 71106
(318) 688-8045
bpsermon@bellsouth.net

For more information:

Visit us @ www.blackpreachersermon.com